if you're

clueless

about

getting a

great job

and

want to

know more

SETH GODIN

BETH BURNS

Dearborn
Financial Publishing, Inc.®

If You're Clueless about Getting a Great Job and Want to
Know More

This publication is designed to provide accurate and authoritative information in regard
to the subject matter covered. It is sold with the understanding that the publisher is not
engaged in the rendering of legal, accounting, or other professional service. If legal
advice or other expert assistance is required, the services of a competent professional person should be sought.

Editorial Director: Cynthia A. Zigmund
Managing Editor: Jack Kiburz
Interior and Cover Design: Karen Engelmann

Published by Dearborn Financial Publishing, Inc.®

Printed in the United States of America

98 99 10 9 8 7 6 5 4 3 2 1

Library of Congress Cataloging-in-Publication Data
Godin, Seth
    If you're clueless about getting a great job and want to know more / Seth Godin
       p.   cm.
    Includes index.
    ISBN 0-7931-2882-X
    1. Job hunting.   2. Career development.   3. Vocational guidance.
4. Success.   I. Burns, Beth.   II. Title
HF5382.7.G62   1998
650.14–dc21   98-5445
                                           CIP

Dearborn books are available at special quantity discounts to use as premiums and sales
promotions, or for use in corporate training programs. For more information, please call
the Special Sales Manager at 800-621-9621, ext. 4384, or write to Dearborn Financial
Publishing, Inc., 155 North Wacker Drive, Chicago, IL 60606-1719.

Other Clueless books by Seth Godin:

If You're Clueless about Mutual Funds and Want to Know More

If You're Clueless about Retirement Planning and Want to Know More

If You're Clueless about Saving Money and Want to Know More

If You're Clueless about The Stock Market and Want to Know More

If You're Clueless about Insurance and Want to Know More

If You're Clueless about Starting Your Own Business and Want to Know More

If You're Clueless about Accounting and Finance and Want to Know More (with Paul Lim)

Acknowledgements

Thanks to Jack Kiburz and Cynthia Zigmund at Dearborn for their invaluable support and guidance; Karen Watts, who continues to be the evil mastermind behind the Clueless concept; and Candyce Norvell, who did a heck of a job pulling it all together.

Thanks, too, go to Heide Von Schreiner, Susan Kushnick, Claire McKean, Shelley Flannery and Rebecca Wald for their top-drawer bookmaking skills. Last, but certainly not least, we appreciate the insight and hard work of the whole crew at SGP, especially Nana Sledzieski, Lisa Lindsay, and Wendy Wax.

Contents

GETTING *a clue* about *getting* A JOB

CHAPTER ONE

When you go out to **look for a job,** you join millions of other people who are doing exactly the same thing. And the question that every **potential employer** will have for you is, "What makes you so **special?**"

If you want to stand out from the crowd and get the job, you had better have a good answer for that question. You need to know what it is you offer that's unique, know how to communicate it, and know how to find the employer who needs what you've got.

This book begins by helping you find out and communicate just what makes you a standout. You'll do it by creating your own personal positioning statement (p.p.s.). Your p.p.s. is a big statement in a small package. It's one sentence—two at the most— that tells you and the whole world who you are and what you can do. This chapter shows you how to create your own p.p.s. step by step. In the process, you'll discover and clarify all kinds of things about yourself as a human being and as a worker:

your goals, your natural talents and abilities, your likes and dislikes, your skills (those that will make you an asset in any job, as well as those that are specific to one job), and more. With the right p.p.s., any employer you approach will know exactly what you have to offer, and you will know right off the bat whether a position is tailor-made for you.

Let's face it. Lots of overworked Human Resources departments are looking for ways to reject people. They are faced with stacks of resumes for only a handful of positions, and everyone who isn't rejected means more follow-up work for them. A focused, directed p.p.s. not only will ensure that you apply for the jobs most suited to you, it will make it dramatically easier to get those jobs.

However, the purpose of this book is not just to tell you how to get a job. It's to tell you how to get the close to ideal job; the job in which you'll be successful, productive, and rewarded. You'll find lots of good, practical information about writing resumes and cover letters, using the Internet to find job openings, learning how to ace an interview, and working with recruiters and every other job-producing tool (short of calling your rich Uncle Henry) available. All of these things can be put to work for you, and this book shows you exactly how to develop a step-by-step method that will maximize your success in the hunt. But it's your p.p.s. that will ensure that these tools are put to the highest use: taking you to the job that's not only perfect, but perfect for you.

By the time you finish this chapter, you'll know exactly what makes you special to employers. The rest of this book will tell you how to find the employer who needs you.

A Brave New World

Whether you have a job but not the right job, or don't have a job at all, there's a lot of good news for you. It's a brave new world for job seekers. It's a world where there are more jobs than there are qualified people to do them. (Depending on where you live, unemployment is probably low to virtually nonexistent.) It's a world where many employers are willing—even eager—to train people who have the right stuff: adaptability; a can-do attitude; assertiveness; and basic teamwork, technology, and communication skills. And it's a world where you can define your own job and blaze your own career path as never before. If you've longed for a flexible schedule, company-paid education, and opportunities to move up, there's never been a better time to get them. If you've dreamed of jumping to a different job or a different industry, such leaps have never been easier than they are right now.

It's not a perfect world. Most people who have really good jobs work really hard at them. Long hours, high performance standards, constant retraining, and long-distance relocations are also common features of the new world. Today's job market is a place where both demands and rewards are high.

Opportunities abound. But in this new, different, and fast-paced world, it can be hard to know how to find the one that's right for you. That's just what this chapter is about. You're going to write your own initial personal positioning statement in two steps. Then you'll edit your initial p.p.s. down to a sentence or two that will be your launchpad to job-seeking success and satisfaction.

Step One: Who Are You, Really?

You'll pour a large portion of your time, energy, and abilities into your next job (as you probably did your last job). That means that a job that doesn't fit will pinch you all day like clothes that are two sizes too small. Maybe you know from painful experience what we're talking about.

MEET JONATHAN

Jonathan is 28 years old and has two years of liberal arts credits. He lost his job at a record company when the company was bought out by an industry giant, but he got a nice severance package that allowed him to take the time to look for the job he's always wanted.

Jonathan's job was designing packaging for cassettes and CDs. (He learned from an older employee on the job, without formal design training, and started out doing old-fashioned "mechanical" layouts, rather than designing and laying out packaging on computer.) He's using the cushion provided by his severance package to take some courses in which he's learning to use popular software such as QuarkXPress and Adobe Photoshop. But Jonathan has no idea what he wants to do next. If you feel a little clueless like Jonathan, you need a p.p.s.

Sample P.P.S.'s

Jennifer, an administrative assistant seeking a similar job with a bigger company: "I excel at assisting others to reach their goals, and have outstanding language, organizational, and technical skills that have enabled me to successfully support two managers who both were promoted during my service."

Teresita is a sales manager seeking to change industries: "I am a people person whose desire to teach and motivate salespeople resulted in a 16 percent increase in sales in my first year at my present job."

Ron is an award-winning fabric designer who has been running his own small business and is seeking a job with a famous fashion designer: "I am a creative person who has combined my artistic talent with merchandising, design, and technology skills to produce award-winning fabric designs for clothing and upholstery."

Step one in creating your personal positioning statement is to figure out who you are as a person, so that this time you can find a job that fits you.

If you're thinking that you don't have the luxury of worrying about finding a perfect fit, let's look at it from the employer's point of view.

Employers don't hire degrees, experience, skills, or achievements. They hire people. While your education, work experience, skills, and achievements all play a role in whether you get a particular job, who you are as a person is very often the determining factor. If there are several applicants who all have the required education and experience, the person who seems to be the best fit for the job and the company will get the job. This is more true today than ever.

So, a person with a job to fill is looking for the person who fits the job. A person with a need for a job is looking for the job that fits who she is. As it turns out, what's best for you is best for the employer. Everybody wants the same thing.

Start with Your Goals

Before you even begin to think about what kind of job you want, take a step back and think about what kind of life you want.

First, think about your goals. Your goals speak volumes about who you are. They are a reflection of what is important to you. Since a job is such a big part of your life, it has to help you reach your important goals.

DON'T JUST READ IT—DO IT!

The exercises in this section will help you clarify your goals. But it's important to actually do the exercises—in writing. The more you put into the process, the more you'll get out of it. So get out a legal pad and a pen, and give some serious thought to the rest of your life!

Write down three short-term goals (say, from now to one year from now), three mid-range goals (one to five years), and three long-term goals (five years and longer). Remember: Think in terms of life goals, as well as career goals.

Finally, write down the one, overarching goal of your life.

If you're not yet clear about what your goals are, now's the time to get clear. One useful way to brainstorm goals is to use the "5 W's" in a new way:

Who? Who do you want to spend your time with? (Answers may include specific people and/or certain kinds of people, such as "creative people" or "people who share my ethical standards.")

What? What do you want to do with your life? (With your time? With your energy? With your talents? With your money?) How do you want to spend your days? What do you want to accomplish or achieve this year, in the next three to five years, and by the end of your life?

When? When do you want to do the "whats?" Do you want to earn another degree now, or wait a few years? When (if at all) do you want to have children? When do you want to retire?

Where? Where do you want to live? (What country? What state? What climate and natural environment? City, suburb, or rural area? What neighborhood?)

Why? (This is an important question, because it may lead you to revise your answers to the other four.)

MORE MONEY!

Everybody can probably guess what some of the highest paying jobs are: movie star, professional athlete, owner of a successful computer company. Here is a sampling of jobs that offer surprisingly better-than-average salaries*:

- Police
  detective $41,018

- Registered
  nurse $38,355

- Police
  officer $34,632

- Electrical
  technician $32,011

- Carpenter $27,102

*Based on median hourly wage for a 40-hour week
(Source: 1996 Nat'l Occupational Employment and Wage Data for Bureau of Labor Statistics)

Why did you answer as you did? Where did you acquire these values and desires? What will the rewards be? Are these really the things that are most important to you? Or, are they goals that have been imposed by others, or by your own limited thinking?

When you know exactly what your goals are, you can make sure you target a job that will help you reach them.

Go Back to Your Old Jobs (Just for a Minute, We Promise)

Make a list of every job you've ever held. Next to each job, list everything you can think of that you liked about it and every way in which it helped you reach a goal. Then, list everything you can think of that you disliked about it, and every way in which it interfered with your goals.

(To trigger your memory, look at the various job aspects listed in "What Is Your Dream Job?" on page eight, and ask yourself whether you liked or disliked that aspect of each job you've had.)

How Do You See Yourself?

Next, think about your interests and preferences. Your answers to these questions will provide pieces to the puzzle that is you.

- Are you most interested in ideas, information, people, or things?

- Are you more interested in helping others, or advancing yourself?

- Do you prefer working with others, or working alone?

- Do you prefer competition, or cooperation?

- Do you like a fast pace, or a slow pace?

- Do you thrive on variety, or routine?

- Do you like to make changes, or maintain the status quo?

- Do you prefer intellectual work, or physical work?

- Do you enjoy and excel at creative work, or rote tasks?

- Do you like to work with details, or the big picture?

- Do you prefer predictability, or uncertainty?

- Do you crave calm, or excitement?

- Do you like to supervise, be supervised, or work independently?

- Do you like a boss who supervises you closely, or who gives you a lot of latitude?

- Do you like a casual environment, or a formal one?

- Do you prefer a set schedule, or a flexible one?

- Are you primarily motivated by money, status, or something else?

What Is Your Dream Job?

Finally, fill out this profile of your dream job, describing each aspect of the job.

I would use these skills   *marketing, technology, diplomacy*

to do this work   *consulting / marketing / finance*

with these kinds of people   *high energy, ambitious*

in this kind of company (industry, size, corporate culture)   *high tech mfg*

in this location   *west coast, Asia*

My commute would be   *< 1 hour*

My schedule would be   *Open*

My work environment would be   *unbounded*

My salary would be   *$90-100K, bonus*

My benefits would be   *vacation, etc*

My level of job security would be   *low to moderate*

My opportunities for advancement would be (based on merit, time served, degrees earned, or other factors? Limited or unlimited?)   *Unlimited*

My boss would be   *open, ambitious, mentoring*

The job's travel requirements would be   *moderate to heavy*

This job would help me reach these goals
in these ways   *challenging job to learn and contribute to a wide range of companies.*

Which Are You?

Below are ten pairs of jobs. Pick the one in each pair that you would rather do. Then look at the ten jobs you've chosen. What do they all have in common? What is it that appeals to you about each job? What skills do they require? Look, too, at all the jobs you didn't choose. Analyzing your "yeas" and "nays" will help you figure out just who you are and what kind of job will fit.

Forest ranger	Bicycle courier
Steel worker	Attorney
Psychologist	Fashion designer
Writer	Actor
Brain surgeon	Airline pilot
Farmer	Car salesperson
Mail carrier	Computer programmer
Accountant	Home builder
Nurse	Public relations executive
Restaurant manager	Lab technician

How Do Others See You?

Your view of yourself is valuable, but not complete. And if you ask other people what they think of you, you may not get a completely honest answer. If you have one of

those friends who always speaks the bald-faced truth, no matter how painful it is to hear, by all means ask her opinion. But you can also get a good idea of how others see you by reflecting on what they say about you without being asked.

- What do people often compliment you about?
  Smarts, sense of humor, unique perspective, organized
- What do people often tease you about?
  Opinated, aloof, different
- What kinds of help do people seek from you?
  Career, finance, human relations
- To whom do people compare you?
  Someone they respect
- How do people describe you to others? For example, when you meet a friend of a friend, the person says, "Jerry has told me so much about you. He says you're so...." *Different*

Bring It Back Around

It's time to take everything you've just learned about yourself and begin turning it into your p.p.s. Remember, your p.p.s. tells who you are and what you can do. Its purpose is to lead you to the job that is perfect for you.

So, the first part of your p.p.s. tells who you are. It should tell the two or three things about you as a person that you think are most important or significant—the things that really stand out about you. These points may have come up in your answers to one of the exercises you just did. More likely, they are points that came up—perhaps in slightly different words—more than once. And the combination of characteristics that you choose to describe who you are is one of the things that will make you stand out to employers. When you find the right job for you, the person who is about to hire you will hear you say these things about yourself and say to himself, "This is the right person for this job."

Okay, so who are you? Look back at your answers in the previous sections. Focus on the ones that stand out—the ones that speak loudest about who you are. Turn those answers into one sentence that tells who you are. That's part one of your initial personal positioning statement.

Step Two: What Are Your Skills?

Next, your personal positioning statement needs to tell what you do. Part of what you do can be stated in terms of skills. Here the phrase to know is "transferable skills." This simply means skills you have that you can transfer to another job or even another career. Transferable skills are not specific procedures but practical abilities you have developed through experience and, sometimes, training. These are the skills that are much in demand in today's fluid job market.

Go through the following skills lists carefully. Think not only about skills you have used on the job but about those you have developed in volunteer work, in educational settings, and in everyday life. You will probably find that you have more skills than you realize. For example, if you have never held a management position, you may not have had an opportunity to develop organizational skills at work. But if you've organized an annual charity walkathon the past three years in a row, you have proven organizational skills. These same skills will transfer to the workplace.

Elaborate a little on each skill that you have. Jot down a few examples of how you have used each one. Write down specifics wherever possible. For example, if using technology is one of your skills, list the kinds of technology you use.

JONATHAN'S INITIAL P.P.S., PART ONE

After assessing himself, Jonathan decided that he is someone who is very interested in both information and people, and someone who prefers a relaxed atmosphere.

He realized that people often ask him to help them understand new technologies. (For example, he gets lots of requests to set up and troubleshoot VCRs and stereo systems.) He also realized that he likes learning about all the different systems and models and using his knowledge to help others feel more comfortable with technology.

Here is part one of Jonathan's initial p.p.s.: "I am someone who likes working with information, technology, and people in a relaxed atmosphere."

Character Counts

One of the things that defines who you are is your character. And when it comes to landing a job, character counts.

When a human resources expert was asked what today's employers were looking for, her first answer was "dependability, dependability, dependability." Employers are looking for people they can count on to show up for work every day, on time, and do the job.

Here are some other much-desired character traits:

- **A can-do attitude backed up by action.** Be willing to work hard, learn new skills, adapt to new ways of doing things, and do whatever it takes to get the job done.

- **An ability to get along.** Be able to get along with other people—even difficult people.

- **Humility.** Be willing to take direction and constructive criticism. When you need help or make a mistake, admit it.

- **Enthusiasm.** Show that you really want the job. Once you get it, show that you really want to *do* the job.

- **Integrity.** Do the right thing. Tell the truth. Keep your word. That sort of thing.

Which of these character traits are strengths you already have? Which ones do you need to work on?

Finally, be honest with yourself about your level of mastery of each skill. Don't over-state what you can really do. You'll use the notes you make about your skills to help you write your p.p.s. and your resume, so it's important to be accurate. Employers are relying on you to tell them honestly what you can accomplish in your new role.

Language skills:

- Speaking—talking with individuals, public speaking

- Writing—correspondence, reports, explanations, proposals, and so on

- Editing *— reviewing tech papers, marketing reports, speeches,*

- Reading *— Business papers/mgs, industry & tech journals*

People skills:

- Greeting

- Mentoring

- Entertaining

- Helping

- Teaching

- Counseling

- Interviewing

- Recruiting

- Negotiating

- Motivating

- Persuading

- Controlling

- Selling

- Promoting

Intellectual skills:

- Learning

- Understanding

- Analyzing

- Applying

- Synthesizing

- Evaluating

- Predicting

- Estimating

- Researching

- Creating

- Problem solving

- Budgeting

- Calculating

Organizational skills:

- Supervising

- Organizing

- Planning

- Managing

- Delegating

- Pricing

- Scheduling

Physical skills:

- Constructing

- Repairing

- Operating (vehicles and machinery)

Scientific skills:

- Testing

- Measuring

- Inspecting

- Using technology

Step Three: What Is Your Experience?

Your experience is what you have done with your skills: how you acquired them (your educational experience), how you have used them, what you have accomplished with them.

You don't tell what your experience is by listing your previous jobs (although you will need to do that, too, later). You tell what your experience is by telling about your actions and accomplishments.

For each skill you marked, write one sentence telling how you put the skill into action, and one sentence telling what the action accomplished. (You may want to write more than one action/accomplishment statement for some skills.)

For example:

Skill

1. Negotiating

2. Writing

3. Problem solving

Action

1. Negotiated with supplier for lower prices and better terms

2. Wrote a new direct-mail campaign for our least-popular product line, which resulted in a 40 percent increase in sales for the line

3. Established and implemented a new system for processing customer refund requests

Accomplishment

1. Reduced cost of materials by 2 percent

2. Increased sales of the line by 13 percent

3. Reduced complaints about slow refunds by 38 percent

Notice that all the accomplishments are quantified. Accomplishments should often (but not always) be stated as a fact, figure, or percentage. Also, accomplishments most often involve increasing something (sales, profits, production, and so on) or decreasing something (customer complaints, employee turnover, costs, and so on).

Now you have the raw material for part two of your initial personal positioning state-

ment. Remember, this is the part that tells what you can do. Imagine that you are sitting in the office of the person who has the power to hire you for your dream job. You have only one sentence to tell him what you can do. It must be a sentence that showcases your unique combination of skills and accomplishments. That's the kind of sentence you want part two of your p.p.s. to be.

Look back over your skills and experiences. Pull out ones that speak of your greatest strengths and accomplishments, and list them. Use them to craft a sentence that tells clearly and powerfully what you do. By focusing your p.p.s. on your strengths, you will automatically be targeting jobs that require these same skills. You will be happier in your new job because your work will showcase your best assets, and your new boss will be ecstatic to find someone who can excel in the job because they have the exact traits required, and have them in spades!

Here are sentences three other job seekers came up with:

- Jennifer is an administrative assistant whose job goal is to work for a top executive at a Fortune 500 company.

  "I have outstanding language, organizational, and technical skills that have enabled me to provide full support to two managers who both were promoted during my service."

- Teresita is a career-changer who wants to do a similar job in a different industry. She has experience as a sales manager for an appliance store and wants to move into sales management at a car dealership.

  "I have a proven ability to teach and motivate salespeople to achieve increased sales, as sales increased by 16 percent in my first year as sales manager at my present job."

ACTION VERBS

Here are some verbs you can use to describe how you have applied your skills:

- Created
- Designed
- Established
- Identified
- Implemented
- Produced

- Ron is a fabric designer who has been running his own small business. His designs have won two industry awards. He is seeking a job with a famous fashion designer.

"I combine my experience in merchandising with state-of-the-art design and technology skills to produce award-winning fabric designs for clothing and upholstery."

Step Four: Write Your Final P.P.S.

JONATHAN'S INITIAL P.P.S., PART TWO

Jonathan decided that his strongest skills are speaking, helping, teaching, learning, understanding, and using technology.

After taking inventory of his skills and experience, Jonathan wrote Part Two of his initial p.p.s.: "I quickly learn how to use new technologies and help others to understand them and feel comfortable with them."

Now, edit your two-part initial p.p.s. down to one or two sentences that clearly tell who you are and what you can do. Write it down. Memorize it. Recite it to your friends. Make it your job-seeking mantra. Let it guide everything you do, from now until you're comfortably settled in your new job.

How Does All This Make You Valuable?

You know who you are and what you can do. Now you need to know what industries and companies need you, your skills, and your accomplishments. To find out, you'll need to do some research.

Keep in mind: You're not looking for a job yet. You're looking for industries and companies that need what you've got.

Do Your Research in Three Stages

You can narrow down your research by looking into those industries, fields, and companies that you know you are interested in. But be careful not to limit yourself too much too soon. Don't overlook an opportunity in an unexpected place. If you're an artist who loves helping people, it's probably safe to rule out accounting. But if you ruled out health care at the get-go, you might never find out about a growing field called art therapy.

Stage One: Get the Big Picture

Read general business magazines and newspapers, such as *The Wall Street Journal, Barron's, Business Week, Forbes, Fortune,* and *Nation's Business.* You'll get an overview of the industries you're interested in. For an even better idea about which specific industries are growing, read *The Employment Outlook: 1994–2005,* a government publication that lists the fastest-growing industries and sectors. Trade magazines (magazines marketed directly to a particular industry, such as *AdvertisingAge*) are one of the best sources of information for job seekers who have narrowed their choices to one or two fields. Some trade magazines are available on newsstands, others you will find out about by talking to people in the industry or searching the Internet. You should come away with the names of one or two industries, and maybe a few specific companies, that seem to need you and your skills.

Stage Two: Research Specific Industries That Interest You

Read about these industries' histories and learn about current trends and forecasts. Be on the lookout for information that confirms that your skills are needed. And, at this stage, start talking to people in your chosen fields.

JONATHAN'S FINAL P.P.S.

Here are the two parts of Jonathan's initial p.p.s.: I am someone who likes working with information, technology, and people in a relaxed atmosphere. I quickly learn how to use new technologies and help others to understand them and feel comfortable with them.

Jonathan's final p.p.s.: "I am an informal person who excels at learning how to use new technologies and helping others to understand and use them."

Here are some specific questions you should try to answer:

- What is happening in this industry? Is it growing, shrinking, or holding steady?

- What kinds of changes is the industry undergoing? Is new technology changing the way things are done? Are existing products and services becoming obsolete? Are new products and services being developed? Are markets expanding? Is competition from overseas firms increasing?

- What kinds of job opportunities exist in the industry now, and what kinds of opportunities will exist in the near future?

- Where is this industry concentrated? In a particular region of the country? In large metropolitan areas?

- What are the leading companies in the industry? Which companies are the largest, which are the fastest growing, which are the most profitable?

Here are some places to find the answers. A good public library should have most or all of these resources. You can also search the Internet.

- Back issues of the business publications listed earlier will give you a long view of particular industries. Here's an example of how these publications can work for you, even if you're not seeking a traditional corporate job.

- *Moody's Industry Review* (Moody's Investors Service, Inc.) is an annual publication that gives financial information about thousands of companies in nearly 150 different industries.

- *The Directory of Industry Data Sources* (Ballinger Publishing Company) is a directory of sources of information about 65 industries. Sources listed include periodicals, market research surveys, databases, and more.

- *National Trade and Professional Associations of the United States*

(Columbia Books, Inc.) is an annual directory of trade and professional associations. Associations whose members work in the industry you are interested in can be a good source of information about trends and careers in the industry.

- *The Career Guide: Dun's Employment Opportunities Directory* (Dun's Marketing Services, Dun & Bradstreet, Inc.) tells what kinds of jobs are available in different industries.

- *Middle Management Report* (E. C. W. Wyatt Data Services) is an annual publication that gives information about middle-management positions in thousands of companies classified by industry. The report gives job descriptions and information about compensation.

Put Industry Insiders to Work for You

After you've learned enough about an industry to confirm your interest and come up with specific questions, begin looking for people who do the kinds of jobs you're interested in. These people will be more willing to spend their valuable time helping you if they can see that you've already taken the time to learn something about the industry. This shows them that your interest is serious and that you'll be asking knowledgeable questions—not wasting their time. People who love their jobs almost always enjoy talking to other people who are also enthusiastic about their field.

Many people find it difficult to call someone on the phone and ask for a favor, especially if the person is a stranger. Here are some ways to make it easier:

- Always try for a personal connection. Call all your friends and relatives, tell them what kind of people you're looking for and why. It's easier to make that call if you can say, "Our mutual friend Amir gave me your name and said you might be willing to talk to me...." You may know someone who knows someone, and the connection you finally make may be somewhat distant, but it's still better than nothing.

- If that fails, try for someone at a business where you are a customer. If

you're thinking about a career in animal care, chances are you're the kind of person who has pets and visits a veterinarian. You already have a relationship with this person; you're just asking to expand its boundaries a bit.

- If you have to approach someone you have no connection to at all, you may want to write a letter first, explaining what you want and why you chose to approach this person. Say that you will call in a few days to see if there's a time when the person would be willing to talk with you on the phone. If the conversation goes well, you may want to try to schedule an in-person meeting. It isn't always necessary to meet with the most visible person in your field. These people are the most likely to be too busy for someone like you. Instead, try asking for an interview with the big fish's rising competitor. You will be more likely to be noticed.

- Always be sensitive to your resource person's schedule and needs. Ask when is a good time for them to talk or to meet, and where. Offer to buy them breakfast or lunch, if that's a convenient time for them. Ask how much time they can spare (or tell them how much time you need, and ask if that's possible). Almost always, the meeting should be no longer than 30 to 45 minutes. Show up on time. Be prepared with specific, educated questions. Take as much time as you asked for, and no more. If things go well, you might ask if the person would mind if you call in the future if you have another question. If it seems appropriate, you could take a small gift, such as a batch of homemade brownies or a pound of gourmet coffee.

- Another good way to approach someone is to offer a trade. Offer to act as an unpaid assistant for a day (or even longer) in return for the opportunity to watch the person work and ask questions. (Most people are more likely to agree to such an arrangement if they've met you, even briefly. So try for a short meeting before you bring up this idea.) Especially if you have some volunteer, freelance, or part-time experience in the field, you may have skills that will be a big help.

The questions you ask your "human resources" will vary, depending on your field and what you've learned in your background research. But here are some questions that are appropriate in almost any situation:

- How and why did you choose this field?

- How did you get started? What kind of educational and experiential background did you have? What has been your path to your current job?

- If you had the choice to make today, would you still choose this field? Why or why not? What would you do differently?

- What do you like most and least about your job?

- What are your plans for the future in this field?

Especially if you are a career changer, ask about ways to get into the field. If you're a bookkeeper who wants to become a newspaper reporter, ask some reporters, "If I could get a bookkeeping job at a newspaper, is there any chance that I could eventually become a reporter, or would I get pigeonholed as a number cruncher? Would I be better off working somewhere else and trying to get freelance assignments at the paper?" Tell the person about your skills and experiences, and ask how you might transfer them to the new field.

JoAnne's Story

JoAnne had worked for seven years as a medical receptionist and was ready for a change. Her sideline business—catering fancy desserts for special events—was much more rewarding and less stressful. But JoAnne had learned from the part-time business that she didn't want to be a businessperson; she wanted to spend her time baking and making people happy, not bookkeeping.

Here's JoAnne's p.p.s.: "I love working with food and people and have the proven ability to provide gourmet pastry catering for a wide variety of special events."

She began to think of a career as a pastry chef working for an upscale restaurant or resort.

JoAnne didn't know if she'd be able to land such a job on the strength of her self-taught abilities. She knew that there were certain classic procedures and recipes that she couldn't pull off. She also knew that there were special training schools for chefs. She just didn't know exactly where they were, how long the training took, or how much it cost. She had no idea how much money she could expect to make. She wondered how recession-proof a pastry chef's job would be, because she knew that expensive restaurants often folded during economic doldrums.

In short, JoAnne had a lot of good questions. The first place she looked for answers was in major business publications. By searching a year's worth of back issues, JoAnne found two articles about chef training schools and several about resorts and restaurant chains that employ pastry chefs. These articles mentioned three different professional associations for chefs and bakers. JoAnne knew that these associations could provide detailed information about her dream job, and she found their addresses in an almanac.

Once JoAnne was educated about the industry, she felt confident enough to approach some people who had the kinds of jobs she was interested in. Because she had been involved in the food service industry, she knew many people in the food supply and restaurant businesses. She started calling her network and quickly came up with the names of three pastry chefs who were willing to talk with her: two who worked in gourmet restaurants, and one who worked at a nearby resort. She hit it off so well with one of her contacts that she asked if she could spend a day assisting the man in order to get a close-up view of what his job was like. He gladly accepted.

A caveat about personal research: Don't base a job or career decision solely on one person's perspective—or even on three people's perspectives. Individual experiences may not reflect the average experiences of people in a given industry. Use your personal research as a complement to solid library research that will provide the big picture.

Stage Three: Investigate Specific Companies

Now it's time to look into those companies that you uncovered in stage two. Remember, you're looking for companies that need you and what you do.

Ask Uncle Sam

The federal Bureau of Labor Statistics (BLS) is a great source of free or cheap information about the economy, industries, and careers. The BLS provides information on everything from general economic trends to specific jobs.

Publications include:

- *Dictionary of Occupational Titles*

- *Geographic Profiles of Employment and Unemployment*

- *Guide for Occupational Exploration*

- *Occupational Outlook Handbook*

- *U.S. Department of Labor Statistics Employment and Earnings Projections 2000*

For a catalog of BLS publications, write to:

Bureau of Labor Statistics
Inquiries & Correspondence
441 G Street NW
Washington, DC 20212

The BLS is on the Web at http://www.bls.gov

- Search back issues of business magazines to find mentions of companies that interest you.

- Check the company's World Wide Web site. (If you don't have the URL, find the site by searching the Web using the company's name as your keyword or call the company's main number and ask for its URL.) If there is a "jobs available" listing, browse through it to see what skills the company needs, what job titles are used (and what they mean), and how the company is structured.

Finding Information about Specific Industries and Fields

If you are interested in advertising:

Standard Directory of Advertising Agencies (National Register Publishing Co., Inc.) lists thousands of U.S. and overseas ad agencies, including their accounts and billings. There is also a list of agencies specializing in various markets, including finance, medicine, and Spanish markets.

If you are interested in banking:

Polk's Bank Directory, North American Edition (R. L. Polk Co.) lists banks and other financial institutions, including names of officers.

If you are interested in consulting:

Consultants and Consulting Organizations Directory (Gale Research, 1996) lists about 15,000 consultants and consulting companies by industry and location.

If you are interested in federal government careers:

The U.S. Office of Personnel Management, 1900 E Street NW, Washington, DC 20415-0001, provides information about civil service jobs nationwide.

If you are interested in insurance:

Best's Insurance Reports (A. M. Best Co.) provides an analysis of each company, as well as addresses and officers' names. One volume covers Property and Casualty, the other covers Life and Health.

If you are interested in manufacturing:

Thomas Register of American Manufacturers (Thomas Register) is a literal encyclopedia (more than 20 volumes) of manufacturers including company profiles, products, and services. You'll also find the complete product catalogs of many companies.

If you are interested in the nonprofit sector:

Encyclopedia of Associations: National Organizations of the United States (Gale Research) lists more than 20,000 nonprofit organizations of every kind. In addition to basics like officials' names, addresses, telephone numbers, and number of members, listings include information about activities, committees, publications, and conventions.

If you are interested in public relations:

O'Dwyer's Directory of Public Relations Firms (J. R. O'Dwyer Co.) lists about 2,000 firms by specialty, location, and clients.

If you are interested in technology:

Corporate Technology Directory (Corporate Technology Information Services, Inc.) is a four-volume listing of high-tech companies arranged by product, location, and company ownership. Includes sales and revenue figures and names of top officials.

- Request annual reports from companies that interest you. (The report may be available at the company's Web site. If not, you probably will find information about how to request one.) The annual report contains a wealth of information about a company's financial position and future plans. You will also find information about the structure of the company and specific jobs people do there. Just be aware that companies think of these reports as promotional tools and put the best possible spin on all the news. Read between the lines.

- Look at *Dun & Bradstreet Million Dollar Directory* (Dun & Bradstreet, Inc.). It lists information about companies and their competitors.

- Go back to people you used as resources in stage two or talk to other people who work at the companies you're now focusing on. Current employees are expert sources when it comes to finding out how a company is organized, what specific job titles are used, and what they mean.

When you finish your research, you should have a firm grasp of what's going on in one or two industries and in a handful of companies in each industry. You should have identified at least one industry that needs what you do, and several companies within that industry that are especially good markets for what you have to sell.

JONATHAN'S RESEARCH

Jonathan researched the technology industry. He wasn't sure any companies would need both his ability to learn new technologies and his people skills. Like many people, he thought of technology as a cold industry, not people oriented. But he found that fast-growing telecommunications companies are in dire need of people with the skills to make new technologies understandable to potential customers. Jonathan knew that those were exactly the skills he had.

Translating Your P.P.S. into a Job Title

You've studied the job market enough to have a feel for what's out there. You've found some industries and companies that need what you've got. You've given careful thought to what you want in a job. With that information, it's time to focus your thinking even further. It's time to decide what job you're going to go after.

By now, it's likely that you know the job title for your dream job. If not, do a little more research. Go back and read some more about your chosen industry and companies. (Bureau of Labor Statistics publications can be useful at this stage, especially the *Dictionary of Occupational Titles*, found in most libraries. See the sidebar "Ask Uncle Sam.") Reconnect with your industry sources, who can fill you in on job titles and what they mean and steer you to the job you really want to do.

Company Profile

Use this template to gather information about companies you research.

History:
Who founded the company—where, when, and why?
_____

Current Profile:
Where are the headquarters and other major facilities?
_____

What products and services does the company provide?
_____

How much does it produce?
_____

What are its sales, revenues, and profits?
_____

What is the area of operation or distribution?
_____

What is the ownership (public or private)?
_____

Who are the officers and executives?
_____

Who are the customers, clients, or market?
_____

What is the company's position in the industry?
_____

What skills does the company need now?
_____

Forecast:
What are forecasters saying about this company's future?
_____

What skills will the company need in the future?
_____

Jonathan Finds the Job Title That Matches His P.P.S.

When Jonathan looked at his final p.p.s. on paper, he was a little worried. He knew immediately one kind of job that was available that partly fit his p.p.s., because he had read a lot about it in his research. The job titles were technical writer and technical editor. Many companies, he knew, needed more people to produce the manuals and other materials that teach buyers how to use technology. They were even looking for people who knew the very software programs that Jonathan had just learned to use. The problem was that Jonathan didn't have writing or editing skills, or any desire to learn them.

People person that he is, Jonathan started talking to his considerable network of friends about his p.p.s. and his problem. And it wasn't long before his networking led to a solution. Jonathan's friend Gale had a friend named Maria who worked in Human Resources (HR) at a large telecommunications company. Maria was always telling Gale that she could never find enough good candidates to fill all the company's openings for customer care representatives. These are people who spend all day talking customers through technology problems on the phone. And Maria always complained that there just aren't that many people who have good technology skills and good people skills.

When Jonathan read his p.p.s. to Gale, Gale thought of Maria and her problem. Gale gave Maria's phone number to Jonathan, and the two of them turned out to be a match made in HR heaven. But we're getting ahead of our story.

Stepping Up the Ladder

Maybe you've known all along what job you want to do because it's your boss's job (or another job within your current company or industry, a level or two above your current job). But you're not sure how good your chances for a promotion are, or how to go about improving them. Maybe you thought (hoped?) you'd have that better job by now and don't understand why you're stuck.

Many people assume that if they do a good job, they'll get promoted to a better job. But it's not that simple. Here are some reasons why you may not have gotten that promotion.

- Your boss has no idea you want it. Some employees don't want more responsibility, even if it means more money. Don't expect your boss to know that you do unless you say so.

- Your company is in trouble, or facing major changes (a downsizing or merger, for example). No matter how stellar your performance is, if the company is struggling, promotions may be on hold, or severely limited. The job you want may even be slated for elimination.

- Your boss doesn't like you. This is not the same thing as your boss thinks you don't do a good job. It's possible to do a fine job, receive strong performance reviews, and still be denied a promotion over personality issues. If your boss doesn't like you as a person, he doesn't want to see you succeed, and he certainly doesn't want you as a peer.

- Your coworkers don't like you. If your boss is savvy to office politics, she's not going to promote someone who's unpopular. She knows people will blame her for giving you more authority. And she also knows that people who don't like you won't perform well for you.

ODD JOBS

Here are some unusual jobs that people really do:

- Toy tester

- Professional golf caddy

- Cowboy/cow-girl

- Lumberjack

- Crime scene cleanup person

- You are isolated. Maybe you're the type who believes in staying to your-self and keeping your nose out of other people's business. Unfortunately, that leaves you out of the loop. No one tells you what's going on, much less asks your opinion of it. You're not seen as a team player. And, gen-erally, the higher up the ladder you go, the more being a team player matters.

- You are doing a thankless job that no one else wants, and you're doing it well. Your boss knows that if he promotes you, he'll have a hard time finding someone else to do your crummy little job as well as you do.

- Your skills are adequate for your current job, but just adequate. You haven't prepared yourself for a better job by learning new skills, getting a degree, or whatever.

Your chances of being promoted increase if:

- You let your boss know what job you want, and find out what you have to do to get it.

- Your company is growing and thriving, and your department is con-tributing to the company's success. (This, obviously, is outside your con-trol. If things look bleak and promise to stay that way, you probably should consider leaving the company.)

- You do what you can to ensure that your boss likes you. In some cases, it just isn't going to happen. But in other cases, a little effort pays off.

- Your coworkers like you. Ditto.

- You get into the flow of office communication and office life. Encourage people to keep you filled in on what's going on, and to seek your advice, counsel, and opinions.

- You have groomed someone to do the routine parts of your job. Your boss is more likely to let you go if she is confident that someone else can step in and do your job as well as you have.

- You have all the skills you'll need to do the job you'd like to have, and you can prove it. The proof may consist of a certificate showing that you've completed a training course. Or it may be a more practical matter of taking on a special project that gives you an opportunity to showcase your abilities.

As with everything else in life, timing is everything. When you've just completed an important project and all the other indicators are positive, ask for the promotion you want. If you don't get it, it may be time to make a change.

Changing Careers

We all know them: those fortunate people who knew at age four what they wanted to be when they grew up, trained to enter their chosen field, and began a seemingly effortless, profoundly satisfying rise through the ranks. Those are the people whose personal positioning statements were, apparently, inscribed on their chromosomes.

Then there are the rest of us. That includes people who make an early career choice and stick with it, but find neither satisfaction nor success because their first choice wasn't an informed choice. And it includes people who make a choice, and then another choice, and then another choice, never committing to one path long enough to gain any ground. Finally, there are all the people in the middle, more or less satisfied, more or less successful, more or less committed.

If you're less rather than more, you're far from alone. Changes in the way companies do business—more outsourced jobs, more part-time jobs, and heavier workloads for the remaining full-timers—have left a lot of workers stressed out, frustrated, and searching for greener pastures. According to the federal Bureau of Labor Statistics, 10 percent of all American workers change careers every year. That may not sound like much, until you realize that 10 percent a year means up to 50 percent over five years.

HEADS UP

Find out what the average compensation package is for the job you're seeking. Check classified ads or professional associations.

Fastest-Growing Careers

(And average entry-level salaries)

• Accountants	$31,000
• Chemical engineers	$44,000
• Computer engineers	$40,000
• Electronics/electrical engineers	$40,000
• Elementary teachers	$23,000
• Financial analysts	$31,500
• Information systems managers	$35,000
• Marketing managers	$28,000
• Physician assistants	$53,000
• Special-education teachers	$25,000

But it's not just external change that pushes people out of one career and into another. There are internal factors, too. Most people are different at age 30 or 40 than they were at 18 or 20, when they made their initial career decisions. You live, you learn, you grow, you change. The job that fit you at age 20 or 25 may not fit you at all at age 35 or 40. In one study, 45 percent of all executives who were looking for jobs wanted to change fields.

If you've changed, or your world has changed around you, it may be time to consider a career change. If you're not sure, look to your personal positioning statement. If your p.p.s. tells you that your current or most recent job didn't even come close to fitting who you are, what you do, and what you can do, you need a new career. That could mean a different kind of job in the same company, or a different kind of job in a whole new industry.

Obviously, a career change is a bigger change than a job change. Here are some things you need to consider if you are thinking about changing careers:

- *Health:* A career change can be a major stress event, depending on how big the change and how many areas of your life are affected. If you have other major changes going on in your life, or a crisis of any kind, now is probably not the time to change careers, too. Wait until your physical and emotional health is strong and your mind is clear. You'll make a better career-change decision and have the inner resources you need to see it through.

BIG CITIES WITH THE MOST NEW JOBS

(Over the next eight years)

- Metropolitan Los Angeles: 877,000

- Atlanta: 641,000

- Houston: 540,000

- Phoenix/Mesa: 504,000

- Dallas: 495,000

- Washington, DC: 479,000

- Seattle: 384,000

- San Diego: 380,000

- Chicago: 350,000

- Minneapolis/ St. Paul: 343,000

How to Change Gears without Stalling

To minimize cuts in job level
and pay when you change careers:

- Learn everything there is to know about the new career so
  you sound like an old pro. Read industry publications and—
  very important—talk to people who are industry veterans.
  Find yourself a mentor.

- Get some part-time, freelance, consulting, or even volunteer
  experience in the industry. Experience in the field should
  translate into a better first full-time position.

- Look for a side door into the industry. Maybe you want to get
  into international marketing. Maybe most of the people com-
  peting with you for jobs have M.B.A.s, and you don't. But
  maybe you spent a year traveling in southern Africa after college, and you know businesspeople there. Find a company
  that's looking to expand its market to southern Africa, and
  you just may find a welcome mat. If there's a credential you're
  lacking, try to find a benefit you can offer that might offset it.

- Take the job nobody else wants. You don't want to take a
  dead-end job. But consider taking a good job in a bad location—for a couple of years. Use the opportunity to show what
  you can do. Accomplish something specific and impressive.
  Then use that accomplishment to get yourself out of Skunk
  Tail, U.S.A. The generalization: Look for a job that has some
  pluses but one minus that's keeping the competition away.
  Use the job to establish yourself in your new career.

- Geography: Changing careers may mean you need to move.
  If you live in Denver and have decided to fulfill your lifelong
  dream of being an oceanographer, start packing.

- *Time:* Changing careers will take time. You will need to research different careers, perhaps get additional education or training, and maybe even try out different careers by volunteering, interning, and so on.

- *Priorities:* Changing careers may mean a change in priorities. If you have been saving money to buy a house or planning to have another child, such changes may need to wait until after your career change.

- *Education:* Changing careers may mean you need to get a degree, take training courses, or get on-the-job training.

- *Money:* Changing careers may mean a temporary or permanent change in how much money you make. If you have to take time off to go to school, or take a low-paying internship or entry-level position, your income could drop drastically. If you choose to enter a lower paying field, the drop could be permanent.

- *Support:* Changing careers means you'll need the support of anyone who will be affected by all the changes that go along with such a move. You may need a spouse to contribute more income, to postpone certain plans, or to make a long-distance move. Those are major changes that require lots of planning and compromise.

- *Age:* Your age should rarely be a barrier to having the career you want to have. In some cases, it is. In the life of every man, there comes a day to reckon with the reality that he will never have a career in professional sports. More often, age is not a barrier but an obstacle that can be overcome only with determination. Sometimes the obstacle

HEADS UP

Good news for career changers: Many companies are looking for people who have transferable skills—communications skills and the ability to open up new markets are two much-mentioned ones—especially for management-level.

is an employer who prefers younger workers who may be willing to work for less. (Legal or not, it happens.) Sometimes the obstacle is more personal. More and more people are starting medical school when they're over 30, or even 40. It can be done. But these students need terrific physical and mental stamina and a willingness to live like college students while their peers are buying bigger houses and taking expensive vacations. Older students will also have fewer earning years in which to repay student loans. Think of the implications of your career change in light of your life stage.

Finally, make sure, before you commit yourself to a career change, that your career is really what needs to be changed. If you're exhausted all the time and blaming it on your job, have a thorough health checkup to make sure there's not a physical cause. If you're insisting on leaving the big city to take up catfish farming and your whole family hates the idea, maybe you need to work on the family problems first.

Forward, March!

Whether you're seeking a new job or a whole new career, it's time to begin your campaign. You know where you're going. Now you can plan your route. In chapter two, you'll make a plan and become committed.

YOU'VE got to be COMMITTED

CHAPTER TWO

*The most important part of your job search is done. Your p.p.s. will shape and direct every facet of your job search, from your resume to interviews. The next step is to get **organized** and get **committed.***

You're launching a campaign whose outcome will affect not only the rest of your career but the rest of your life. It's important to outline your strategy and commit yourself to it. Be prepared to stay the course until you reach your goal.

Set Up Your Command Center

You need a place from which to launch your campaign—your command center, you might call it. Set up your command post in a territory you can claim as your own for the duration of your job search. It can be a corner or a closet, as long as it's quiet and it's yours. (The dining room is not a good choice. You'll be in the way at mealtime. Your resume will get gravy-stained.)

Working Double-Time

If you're looking for a new job while still employed:

- Don't look for a job while you're at work.

- Don't tell anyone at work that you're job-hunting.

- Don't change old habits in ways that will give you away. For example, don't change the way you dress for work or take extra long lunch hours.

- Don't give potential employers your work number. They should appreciate your desire to devote your full attention to the job you're being paid to do. On the other hand, if they see that you're willing to job-hunt on your current employer's time, they have every reason to expect that you would be willing to treat them the same way.

Furnish your command center with a desk or table, a word processor or computer, a phone, a place to keep paperwork safe and organized, a planning calendar, and basic office supplies. Write your p.p.s. in big block letters and put it on the wall where you can see it.

Though experts highly recommend that you get a telephone line that is dedicated to your job search, it is unlikely that many people can or would do so. At the very least, you need a line that will always be answered by you or by a professional-sounding voice mail or answering machine message. If you have access to voice mail, use a separate mailbox for your job search.

Plan Your Campaign

Now you're ready to make a plan: to write down all the things you need to do to turn your p.p.s. into reality, and *schedule* when you're going to do them.

Plan a four-month job campaign. It may take longer. It may take only four weeks. But four months is a good average. Map out a general, long-term plan. Then, plan each week and each day in detail.

Long-Term Goals: Giant Steps to Your New Job

Begin by making a table with columns labeled Month 1, Month 2, Month 3, and Month 4.

Obviously, your ultimate goal is to land a job that matches your p.p.s. Write that in, along with monthly goals that will get you there. Here's a sample showing how your overall plan might look:

*P.P.S.:*_____

*Objective:*_____

(Example: Obtain a job as a fashion designer with a top firm)

P.P.S.: I am a creative person who has combined my artistic talent with merchandising, design, and technology skills to produce award-winning fabric designs for clothing and upholstery.

Objective: Fabric design and production position with a world-class fashion design firm desiring to produce unique, hand-applied fabric designs.

Tasks to complete:

Month 1

- Finish this book.

- Gather information for resume.

- Line up references.

- Prepare personal appearance and wardrobe.

- Write resume and cover letter.

- Identify employers to contact.

- Identify employment agencies and search firms to contact.

- Schedule appointments with agencies and search firms.

- Brainstorm networking contacts and activities.

- Schedule at least eight networking activities.

- Continue library and personal research.

- Research companies online.

- Begin mailing out resumes.

- Begin making telephone contacts with employers.

Month 2

- Continue library, personal, and online research.

- Schedule at least ten networking activities.

- Mail out at least 80 resumes.

- Follow up on at least 40 job leads.

- Have at least eight interviews.

- Make follow-up calls as needed.

Making Contact: Who Can You Add to Your Network?

Here are some places to find people to add to your network:

- Family

- Friends

- Neighbors

- Coworkers (past and present)

- People you know through hobbies or community activities

- People who are part of your religious community

- People whose services you use (doctor, dentist, veterinarian, lawyer, accountant, insurance agent, and so on)

Month 3

- Continue library, personal, and online research.

- Schedule at least ten networking activities.

- Mail out at least 50 resumes.

- Follow up on at least 40 job leads.

- Have at least eight interviews.

- Make follow-up calls as needed.

The Numbers Game

How many resumes you mail, calls you make, and interviews you have each week will vary depending on your industry, the position you're seeking, and so on. But here are some averages experts say you should shoot for:

- Mail 10 to 25 resumes a week. (You'll probably send out more resumes per week early in your job search.)

- Make 40 to 50 calls a week (first contacts, follow-ups, information seeking, and so on).

- Schedule two to four interviews a week. (This number probably will be higher later in your job search than it is early on.)

Month 4

- Continue library, personal, and online research.

- Schedule at least ten networking activities.

- Mail out at least 50 resumes.

- Follow up on at least 40 job leads.

- Have at least eight interviews.

- Mail out 50 resumes.

- Make follow-up calls as needed.

A Template for Your Plan

P.P.S.:

_____
_____
_____

Objective:

_____
_____

Month _____
Tasks to Complete

_____
_____
_____
_____
_____
_____

Week _____
Tasks to Complete

_____
_____
_____
_____
_____

What to Do When Your Plan Isn't Working

 If you've mapped out a plan but you're not making progress in your job search (i.e., you've been at it for two months and you don't have a single interview scheduled), here are some questions to ask yourself:

- **What are my numbers?** The best plan in the world won't work if you don't actually carry it out. How many phone calls are you making each week? How many resumes are you sending out? (If you don't have records that tell you the answers, that's Problem No. 1.) Compare your numbers to those in the sidebar "The Numbers Game." If your numbers are low, increase your production!

- **Am I doing something wrong?** Sit down with a couple of people you trust and go over your plan, your resume and cover letter, your methods of finding job leads, a list of leads you are pursuing, and every other aspect of your job search. Ask these people for an honest critique. Do they see anything that could be ambushing your efforts? For example, do you need to rewrite your resume or are you pursuing jobs for which you're underqualified? Sometimes an objective observer will see problems that you have missed. If your informal counselors can't pinpoint the problem, you may want to consult a certified career counselor. (See chapter seven, "Who's After Your Head?" for more information about certified career counselors.)

- **Is there a problem with my references?** If you see a pattern of employers asking for your references and then losing interest in you, you need to check your references yourself. Call and ask them which employers have contacted them and if they know of any reason why the employers may have lost interest. If you have any reason at all to believe that a reference is not being 110 percent positive about you, take that person's name off your reference sheet.

Mid-Range Goals: What Are You Going to Do Next Week?

Now, break each month down into weeks and schedule five-day job-hunting weeks. Put high-priority goals early in each week's schedule. Next week's priorities are to assemble the tools you need to begin your job search: your resume, wardrobe, and so on.

Short-Term Goals: What Are You Going to Do Tomorrow?

Make a to-do list for each job-hunting day. Some people like to make their lists the night before; others do it first thing every morning. Make your list specific: specific people to call, specific people to whom to mail resumes, and so on. After you've made your list, rank each item in order of importance and give the more important items priority. Tackle them as early in the day as possible. Generally, it's best to make phone calls in the morning.

Presenting Yourself as an Asset

When you're looking for a job, it's natural for you to be thinking about what an employer can do for you. After all, you need a paycheck. Most likely, you want a nice benefits package, a job title with some prestige, and a chance to do what you're good at and enjoy doing. There's nothing wrong with any of that. But you don't get what you want by asking for it. (Life is never that simple.) You get what you want by convincing employers that you are what they want.

NETWORKING OPPORTUNITIES

Where can you network? Any place where people are gathered for social or business purposes is a place where you can network. But if you're looking for prime networking territory, check out meetings and events sponsored by:

- Business organizations such as the Chamber of Commerce and National Association of Women Business Owners
- Professional or trade associations in your industry
- Alumni organizations

Think about it: An employer has no reason to care what you want, unless you have something she wants. If each of you has something the other wants, the stage is set for a win-win negotiation. To set the stage, you need to present yourself as an asset the employer needs. Every contact you have with potential employers—on paper, online, on the phone, and in person—must reinforce the fact that you are what they need.

An Asset on Paper: Your Resume

Remember, your resume is not about what you want or need. It's about who you are and what you can do that an employer needs.

Imagine that you are a resume screener facing a stack of 200 resumes. Your job is to choose ten applicants who will be interviewed for the two positions available. Would you be more interested in resumes that are about what the applicant wants, or in those that focus on what you, the employer, need?

Chapter three tells you how to write and produce a resume that presents you as a must-see asset.

An Asset Online: Your Electronic Presence

Your online presence—on your own Web site if you have one, on sites where you post your resume, and in every e-mail message you send—is another opportunity to present yourself as an asset. E-mail lets you show that you can quickly compose clear, professionally written communication. (If you can't, you must learn. Good communications skills—written and oral—are among the most sought-after skills of all.) And all your online

HEADS UP

Often, the best time to reach busy managers and executives is before 9 a.m. or after 5 p.m., when secretaries and assistants may not be in to screen their calls. And the best time to reach any business is during its slowest hours. For example, call a restaurant after lunch and before dinner.

communication should focus on what you can do for employers. Chapters five and eight tell you more about presenting yourself as an asset online.

An Asset on the Phone: Your Voice, Your Attitude

Have you ever known anyone who likes to call up people they don't know and ask for things? Probably not. Yet, at one time or another, everybody has to do it. Job-hunting time is one of those times.

Fortunately, the key to making these calls painless is also the key to making them effective. Don't be a beggar. Don't call with the attitude that you are calling to ask for something; call with the attitude that you are calling with something to offer.

Of course, it's likely that you will ask for something—the name of the person who should receive your resume or a personal interview, for example. But whatever you ask for should be secondary to what you're offering. And you know what that is: an asset the employer needs. Your attitude, your tone, and your words should convey that you are someone who has something of value to offer. Be confident, but not cocky. When you talk about yourself, your skills, and your accomplishments, do it in the context of what you can do for the person (and, by extension, the company) on the other end of the line.

An Asset at the Interview: Ms. or Mr. Ambassador

As everybody knows, an ambassador is a person who represents one country in another country. A good ambassador embodies all the best traits of her native land, in order to make a favorable impression on the people in the country where she serves. She is well dressed, well groomed, poised, gracious, cool under fire, and intelligent. She got her job because she is the kind of person her country wants representing it.

Can you guess where this is going? Whatever the job title, every time an employer makes a hire, he is hiring an ambassador. He is looking for someone who is the personification of all the best in his company. He is looking for someone who will fit in with the rest of the "citizens" and also represent the company well in the world at

Inspiration in Your VCR

Here are a few movies that make choice viewing when you need inspiration:

- *The African Queen.* Humphrey Bogart and Katharine Hepburn survive malaria, leeches, torpedoes, and each other.

- *Chariots of Fire.* Based on the true story of British runners Harold Abrahams and Eric Liddell, and their quest for Olympic gold in 1924.

- *Joseph.* The 1995 version from Turner Pictures is dramatic and inspiring. Joseph endures a string of betrayals and defeats that would break a lesser man, sticks to his principles, and wins big.

- *Rocky.* The ultimate underdog movie, it should inspire anybody to fight the good fight.

- *Sense and Sensibility.* Two very different sisters persevere through difficulty and disappointment until they reach their happy endings.

large. If it isn't immediately apparent to him that you will do these things, all the skills and accomplishments in the world won't get you the job. As you think ahead to your interviews, think like an ambassador-to-be.

Chapter eight tells you all about how to present yourself as an asset at interviews.

Committing Yourself to the Process

Job-hunting may be the toughest job you'll ever do. If you don't have a job, gremlins named Insecurity, Self-Doubt, Confusion, Anxiety, Depression, and Outright Fear may be battling for possession of your soul. If you're holding down one job while looking for a better job, at least you still have your identity and your income. But you also have the stress of, essentially, doing two jobs at once and making sure you keep them separate. (See the sidebar "Working Double-Time.")

If you have all the right stuff—an impressive resume, a dazzling Web site, and all the rest—but you yourself crash and burn before you finish the race, it was all for nothing. You are the product. You have to look good and perform well throughout your job-search campaign, in spite of the stress of it all. You need to be mentally tough, emotionally strong, and physically ready. You must be committed to running a good race and making a strong finish. Here's how to do it.

Be Calm and Consistent

You're three weeks into your job search. You know your p.p.s. so well that you're repeating it in your sleep. You know what you want, and you're following your plan to get it.

Then, suddenly, panic strikes. Maybe it comes in the form of an unexpected expense. Or maybe your friend Jamie just got a great job offer after only two weeks of looking. You toss and turn through a sleepless night, your mind running in endless circles like a hamster on a squeaky wheel. You've got to do something!

The next morning, your brother-in-law calls to tell you about a job opening he just heard about. It's not what you really wanted to do…you've never heard of the company…it's a nightmare commute…it wouldn't be a career-track job…but, hey, it's something. And, after all, you need a job!

Okay: What do you do? Turn your p.p.s. into a paper airplane, lower your sights, rewrite your resume, and abandon your plan?

No, you don't. You get ahold of yourself. You take a few deep breaths. You read your

p.p.s. out loud in a firm, confident voice. You calm down and commit yourself to staying on the path you've mapped out.

Why? Because if you go off course in pursuit of your brother-in-law's lead and don't get the job, you've wasted valuable time and resources. And if you do get the job—the job you don't really want and aren't really right for—your whole life is headed off course. How much of your life will you waste in that wrong job before you give up on it (or it gives up on you) and land right back where you are now?

Commit yourself to your p.p.s. and your plan. Stay on the path that leads to your destination.

Be Positive and Persistent

Getting sidetracked is one problem. Getting stalled is another. Just as you can't wander off and explore every detour and side path, you can't just sit idly in the road. You must keep moving forward.

This can be hard to do when you meet with rejection. When a potential employer hangs up on you, when you don't get called for an interview, when you get the interview but not the job—all these are rejections that feel like failures. A string of rejections can sap your motivation, kill your momentum, and leave you wondering, "What's the use?"

When you feel that way, remember that failure is the rule, not the exception. Here's a good example: Once upon a time there was a guy who decided he was cut out for a career in politics. Eight times he ran for various local and state offices, and eight times he lost. *Eight times!* Now, a politician's job is a popularity contest if any job is. And you would think that eight rejections in a row—eight failures—would have been enough to convince this guy that he was not popular. You would think that he would have crawled into a deep, dark hole never to be seen again. But this man was doggedly persistent. He just kept running for office, willing to face still more rejection and failure. Finally, he won an election. Maybe you've heard of him: Abraham Lincoln.

The Keys to Maintaining Enthusiasm

 Here are some strategies to help you stay positive.

- **Schedule at least one thing every day that you will look forward to.** Even if it's just an ice cream cone.

- **Set reachable daily and weekly goals.** You'll maintain momentum as you mark off tasks accomplished and move closer to your big goal.

- **Reward yourself for successes.** Don't wait until you're hired to do something nice for yourself. Give yourself a pat on the back and a soak in the Jacuzzi—or whatever small treat makes you feel good—when your resume is finished, when you've reached all your weekly goals, or when you land your first interview.

- **Keep the input positive.** Avoid people who feel compelled to wag their heads and tell you about the M.B.A. they know who was out of work for seven months and finally joined a flower-selling cult. Spend your time with positive people. Read biographies of people who persevered and achieved their dreams. Rent *Rocky* videos. Listen to your favorite motivational tapes.

- **Remind yourself of past successes and achievements.** Make a list of goals you've set and achieved—large or small. You've done it before; you can do it again. (Flip side: Don't dwell on past defeats and disappointments.)

- **Give yourself a break.** If you have a really bad morning—like, you blew the interview you worked three weeks to get—give yourself the afternoon off. Then start fresh tomorrow.

Then there was the seven-year-old who was so "dumb" that his teacher gave up on him and his mom had to teach him at home. When he grew up, he decided that he was an inventor, and he tried to invent things. The only problem was, his inventions failed over and over. Some of them failed hundreds of times, yet this "dummy" kept trying to make them work. Finally, a few of his projects started to pan out: the light-bulb, the record player, the electric generator. Thomas Edison ended up with more than 1,000 patents to his name.

Why did people like Lincoln and Edison keep trying in the face of so much rejection and failure? Because they knew what they wanted and were determined to get it. They were positive in the face of the negative, and they were persistent.

Be Kind to Yourself

"Take care of yourself" is a cliché. But it's still an important key to a successful job search. You need to take one or two days a week off from looking for a job or even thinking about it. And you need to pamper yourself a little. Make this a time to move toward personal, as well as professional, fulfillment.

Do something you've always wanted to do to take better care of yourself. This should be something that you will find enjoyable and relaxing and that will increase your health and well-being. Don't take on a major self-improvement project that will require an iron will or painful sacrifices. If you're a smoker, quitting would certainly be a boon to your health. But the process won't be enjoyable and will likely entail more stress than you should take on at an already stressful time. The idea here is to do something that feels good, in addition to being good for you.

Here are some possibilities:

- Get in the habit of taking a walk every day.

- Take a class in exercise, dance, yoga, or a martial art. Having someplace to be at a certain time every day will help you structure your time and provide stress-free human contact. (Of course, you may choose to use the class as a networking opportunity. But give yourself permission to be there just for you.)

You Mustn't Quit

When things go wrong, as they sometimes will,
When the road you're trudging seems all uphill,
When the funds are low and the debts are high,
And you want to smile, but you have to sigh,
When care is pressing you down a bit,
Rest! if you must—but never quit.
Life is queer, with its twists and turns,
As every one of us sometimes learns,
And many a failure turns about
When he might have won if he'd stuck it out;
Stick to your task, though the pace seems slow—
You may succeed with one more blow.
Success is failure turned inside out—
The silver tint of the clouds of doubt—
And you never can tell how close you are,
It may be near when it seems afar;
So stick to the fight when you're hardest hit—
It's when things seem worst that you mustn't quit.

—Author Unknown

- If you're among the millions of people who don't get enough sleep and constantly battle fatigue, get in the habit of going to bed an hour earlier. Or, if it doesn't interfere with your job-search schedule, sleep an extra hour in the mornings.

- Kick the junk food habit once and for all. Changing your diet and eating habits is a learning process that takes some time, attention, and effort. Use your relatively flexible job-search schedule to build healthier habits that will work for you now and after you're back on the job.

In addition to the health benefits of your new habit, here are some other payoffs you can expect:

- You'll feel better and look better. Those are personal and professional pluses.

- Because you feel better and look better, you'll be more confident. Another personal and professional advantage.

- You'll gain a sense of accomplishment, a sense of control over your life, a sense that you can do what you set out to do. This, too, will increase your confidence and enthusiasm for the job search.

A RESUME is worth more than the paper it's PRINTED ON

CHAPTER THREE

*Your resume is a brief, focused autobiography that tells **employers** everything they need to decide whether to **interview** you.*

Every potentional employer must decide—sometimes in a matter of seconds— whether you are a strong enough job candidate to merit an interview. No resume can tell employers everything they need to know about you, but it is your most important calling card. It's the tool you use to entice someone to want to know more.

The hard fact is that the first person who reads your resume wants to reject you. Resume readers want to reject as many resumes as possible, because every resume they accept means more work for them and for their superiors: more people to call, more people to interview, more references to check, and so on. Your resume must give readers reasons to accept you; reasons to invest the time and energy to interview you.

Why You Need a Resume

In a sense, your resume is your p.p.s. in an expanded form. Your p.p.s. tells who you are and what you can do. Your resume lays out how you got to be who you are (your educational and work experiences) outlines and documents what you can do by telling exactly what you've done, where, when, and with what results.

But your resume provides employers with much more information about you than the mere facts it lists. It shows how well you are able to distill, organize, and present information. It shows your ability to write clearly and precisely. It says something about your marketing skills. The way you package your resume—the stationery and typeface you use, the quality of printing—makes a statement about your level of professionalism and your quality standards. If your resume provides evidence of weakness in any of these areas, it will work against you. Take the time and make the effort to develop a perfect resume.

What Employers Want to See

An employer who is reading resumes is doing so because he has a problem to solve. There is a job in his company that needs to be done that is not getting done (or, if the position is not yet vacant, will not be getting done for very much longer). He is interested in resumes that say, "I am the person who can solve your problem. I can do the job that needs to be done. I can be an asset to your company."

Keep your resume focused on what you can do for the employer.

Using Keywords

As important as what employers want to see is what their computers want to see. Most large companies and a growing number of mid-size and even smaller companies scan resumes into a computer and use resume tracking software to organize and search them. When a job opens up, someone searches all stored resumes, using certain keywords to find the resumes of people who are qualified for the job.

This means you must make sure that your resume contains the keywords that are commonly used to search for people qualified to do the job you want. If you have and list all the desired skills and experience but don't use the keywords employers use, the computer will skip over your resume; no human being will ever consider your qualifications.

Keywords are almost always nouns; occasionally they are adjectives that describe a desired character or personality trait (aggressive, confident). They may be job titles (for example, administrative assistant, sales manager, textile designer) or department names (Human Resources, Accounts Payable). They may be degrees. (For example, a health care firm searching for a patient counselor may use the keywords "Master of Social Work" or "Certified Marriage, Family, and Child Counselor.") They may be skill names (budgeting, estimating) or even product names, such as the names of software programs that applicants must know.

To find out what keywords you must use for the specific job you want:

- Ask people in your industry who are in a position to know. Possibilities include someone in a Human Resources department or someone who was recently hired.

- Read lots of classified ads for positions like the one you are seeking, and notice what nouns are used consistently in the ads.

- Check sample keyword lists in *Electronic Resume Revolution* by Joyce Lain Kennedy and Thomas J. Morrow (John Wiley & Sons, 1995).

- Consult a recruiter who is active in your industry. That person can be a good source of information about keywords.

There are two ways to get keywords into your resume. One is to make a list of keywords the first item, right after your name, address, and telephone number. A resume that begins with a list of keywords is sometimes called an electronic resume, because it is formatted specifically for electronic searches.

Another way to use keywords is to work them into your objective and/or summary. (In theory, resume search software should find keywords appearing anywhere in your resume. But experts say it's best to place them as high on the page as possible.)

Which method you choose will depend partly on your industry. In a technologically oriented industry, a resume that begins with a list of keywords shows that you're up to speed. However, in a more people-oriented field like education, such a list may be off-putting. Even if the employer uses resume search software and keywords, she may prefer a more traditional resume format. If in doubt, you can always produce two resumes, identical except that the second includes a list of keywords at the top. Then, make your best judgment about which version to send to which employers. Or, if you have an opportunity, ask the employer if the company prefers resumes that include a keyword section. (Most experts say you should not send two versions of your resume to the same company. Whenever you customize your resume be sure that you send only one version to each company.)

Types of Resumes

With or without keyword lists, there are three basic types of resumes. While there are some differences in content among the three, the biggest difference is in how information is organized and presented. The various types of resumes allow you to choose what parts of your background you want to highlight and what parts you want to de-emphasize.

The Chronological Resume

The chronological resume is the traditional standard. It is simply a list of the jobs you've held, with more or less description of exactly what each one involved. Your present or most recent job is listed first, with past jobs following in order, from recent to distant past. As a general rule, a chronological resume covers ten years (if you've been working that long).

Use a chronological resume if:

- You have stayed on a single career path. If you can show a consistent pattern of increased responsibility, so much the better.

- You have been consistently employed, with no significant gaps.

Seven Things to Leave Off the Resume

1. When you can start. This is to be negotiated when you are offered a job. Announcing that you're "available immediately" can make you sound desperate if you're unemployed, or disloyal to your current employer if you have one.

2. Why you're job-hunting. Again, this issue will come up later. You need to be prepared to answer it in an interview, but it doesn't belong on your resume.

3. Anything about money or other compensation issues. Remember, the purpose of your resume is to tell potential employers what you can do for them, not to tell them what you want from them.

4. Lies. (And exaggerations count as lies.) Almost always, you will be found out and disqualified. If an employer gets to the stage of thinking seriously about hiring you, he is likely to check the accuracy of your resume very carefully. It is not unusual for employers to check with educational institutions listed on a resume to confirm that claimed degrees were actually earned. Any claims you make about past jobs (accomplishments, job titles, and so on) may be thoroughly checked out. Employers need your written permission to do this, but if you're hesitant to give it, it will be pretty clear why. And employers also sometimes use informal networks to sidestep possible legal problems in probing an applicant's background. For example, your past employers are limited by law in what they can say about you when asked for a reference. But if a potential employer already employs (or simply knows) someone who worked with you at a past job, she may ask that person about you.

5. Your age, race, and ethnic background or gender. There are laws preventing employers from using your age as a criterion

for employment. They can't ask, so don't tell. Of course, the information you give about your educational and work background will give the employer some idea of your age. But there's no need to be specific or to call attention to this factor.

6. Your health status. Unless you're seeking employment as a professional athlete, it is assumed that you are in generally good health and physically able to do the job you're applying for.

7. Your childhood. If your resume lists a college degree or other advanced education, there's no need to mention that you graduated from high school; it's assumed. (Possible exception: if you went to a prestigious high school, such as a private school recognized for high academic standards.) And there's rarely any reason to include anything that occurred in your life before you turned 18. A resume never, ever begins, "I was born in a log cabin...."

The Chronological Resume Template

Name

Street address; city, state, ZIP; telephone; fax number; e-mail address; Web address

Summary or objective

Experience (chronological order, from most recent to most distant)

Company name, city, and state

Job title, dates of employment

Description of duties and responsibilities

Accomplishment statement

Anatomy of a Resume

Here are brief guidelines for writing your resume, part by part:

Heading

This is your name, street address, city, state, ZIP, and telephone number. Include your fax number, e-mail address, and Web site address if you have them. There are no set rules for format, as long as the information is clear and looks attractive on the page

Objective

Resume writers often go astray here by writing a sentence about what they want. This is an immediate turnoff to the person reading the resume. The purpose of the objective is to let the employer know, as specifically as possible, what job you can do for her. If possible, use a job title.

No: "An opportunity to use my sales and training skills in an industry that offers high income potential."

Yes: "Sales manager position at an auto dealership seeking to increase sales through increased training and motivation of sales staff."

Summary

The summary is a capsule explanation of who you are and what you can do. Sound familiar? Yes, a summary is much like a p.p.s. In some cases, you may be able to use your p.p.s., word for word, as your summary. Or use the same ideas worded slightly differently. (Compare Teresita, Ron, and Jonathan's p.p.s.'s in chapter one to their summaries shown on the sample resumes in this chapter.)

Skills (functional and combination resumes)

Name recognized, transferable skills. (Go back to the skill-listing exercise in chapter one for a list of common skills.) Make sure the skills you list are important to the job you are applying for, and use the names that are commonly used for these skills. Describe how you have used each skill and what you have accomplished in each skill area. (Go back to the accomplishment statements you wrote in chapter one.)

Work (chronological resume)

Describe your most important duties and responsibilities, and name your most important accomplishments. (Use the accomplishment statements you wrote in chapter one as guidelines.) Be as specific as possible. Dates of employment can be placed before the description (next to the job title) for more emphasis, or after the description for less emphasis. To camouflage short gaps in employment, give years only; otherwise, give the month and year of starting and ending dates.

Education

Include any formal education that is relevant to the job. Describe the skills or knowledge you acquired if this is not clear from the title of the course or program. Tell what degree or certification you earned, if any.

Other Information

List any other information about yourself that will interest potential employers. Foreign language proficiency is almost always worth noting if you are truly fluent. One year in high school is not worth mentioning. List professional associations if they are relevant. Mention volunteer work if there is some professional connection; for example, if you use job-related skills in a volunteer capacity. List any industry training such as extra computer skills or any art certificates that you have.

Company name, city, and state

Job title, dates of employment

Description of duties and responsibilities

Accomplishment statement

Company name, city, and state

Job title, dates of employment

Description of duties and responsibilities

Accomplishment statement

Education (chronological order, from most recent to most distant)

Institution name, city, and state

Degree or certification, major field or subject area, date

Description of coursework, skills acquired, and so on if relevant

Other Information (optional; professional associations, relevant volunteer activities, languages, and so on)

The Functional Resume

The functional resume is organized according to your skills, rather than according to your job history. Of course, the skills you list will depend on your industry or field and your individual experience. A functional resume for a corporate manager might list the person's experience in management, sales, finance, and operations. A sales manager's functional resume might list the skill areas sales, sales management, and administration. An accountant might list accounts payable, accounts receivable, and payroll accounting skills.

Sample Resume

Chronological Resume for an Administrative Assistant

Jennifer Doe
1234 Star Avenue
St. Louis, Missouri 66666
(314) 555-5555
e-mail: jenndo@inet.com

Objective:
An administrative assistant position providing support for a senior finance executive at a Fortune 500 company.

Work History:
Black Shoe Company, St. Louis, MO
Administrative Assistant to the Vice President, Finance, Feb. 1990–Dec. 1997

- Compiled, input, proofread, produced, and distributed monthly, quarterly, and annual financial statements. Responsible for all correspondence, scheduling, and travel arrangements for the vice president. Proficient in the use of MicroSoft Excel, Lotus 1-2-3, and Microsoft Word. Transcribe at 110 wpm.

- All financial statements were distributed on time during my service, a company record.

- The vice president I supported was promoted from assistant vice president two years after I became his AA.

Americana Furniture Company, Springfield, IL
Administrative Assistant to the Comptroller, Jan. 1988–Dec. 1989

- Input, proofread, copied, and distributed monthly, quarterly, and annual financial statements. Responsible for all correspondence, telephone support, scheduling, and travel arrangements for the comptroller.

- Computerized financial statements so that part-time typists were no longer needed to help complete them. This resulted in an annual savings of $22,000.

- Comptroller was promoted to vice president.

Americana Furniture Company, Springfield, IL
Secretary to the Finance Department, June 1985–Dec. 1987
- Provided all secretarial support services for the Accounts Payable, Accounts Receivable, and Payroll departments. Duties included data entry, correspondence, telephone support, and computation.

Education:
Central Illinois Junior College, Springfield, IL
Associate's Degree in Office Administration, May 1985

Other:

Computer Age Business College, Springfield, IL
Certificates in Microsoft Excel (Advanced) and Lotus 1-2-3 (Advanced), August 1987

If you don't have solid experience in at least three skill areas that are important in the job you are seeking, a functional resume is not your best choice.

Because a functional resume focuses on your skills, not on the specific jobs you have held, it is important that you include both a clear objective and a well-written summary. The purpose of both is to tell employers what your skills can do for them. The objective should specify what job you are seeking. The summary should tell a potential employer how your unique collection of skills will make you an asset to her company.

Use a functional resume if:

- You have experience in most or all of the main functions or skills required for the job you are seeking.

- You have changed careers in the past or are doing so now. A functional resume will highlight transferable skills that will be as useful in your new career as they were in the old one.

- You are moving from one sector of the economy to another; for example, if you've always worked for nonprofit organizations but want to move into the corporate world, or you're leaving the military and seeking a corporate job. Again, a functional resume highlights transferable skills.

- You have big gaps in your work history or are re-entering the work force. A functional resume de-emphasizes employment dates.

The Functional Resume Template

Name

Street address; city, state, ZIP; telephone; fax number; e-mail address; Web address

Objective

Summary

Skill area: name or description of skill, how you have used it, what you accomplished

Skill area: name or description of skill, how you have used it, what you accomplished

Skill area: name or description of skill, how you have used it, what you accomplished

Skill area: name or description of skill, how you have used it, what you accomplished

Work History

Company name, city, and state

Company description

Job title, dates of employment

Company name, city, and state

Company description

Job title, dates of employment

Company name, city, and state

Company description

Job title, dates of employment

Education (chronological order, from most recent to most distant)

Institution name, city, and state

Degree or certification, major field or subject area, date

Description of coursework, skills acquired, and so on if relevant

Other Information (optional; professional associations, relevant volunteer activities, languages, and so on)

The Combination Resume

The combination resume starts out like a functional resume but beefs up the work history section by adding the descriptions of duties and responsibilities contained in the chronological resume. (Accomplishment statements may be placed in the skill section or the work history section, whichever works best for you.)

All this information will almost certainly expand your resume to two pages. Some experts see this as a disadvantage, believing that a one-page resume is more employ-

Sample Resume

Combination Resume for a Sales Manager

Teresita Mendez
1234 Star Avenue
Miami, Florida 33222
(305) 555-5555
e-mail:tmsalespro@inter.net

Objective:

Sales manager position at an auto dealership seeking to increase sales through increased training and motivation of sales staff.

Summary:

Proven record of training and motivating others to increase sales.

Skills:

Sales management: Experienced manager of a combined full-time/part-time sales staff selling big-ticket retail. Two professional certifications in sales management.

* In my current position as sales manager, overall sales increased 16 percent in my first full year.

Training:

Developed my own training course for the sales staff I supervise, resulting in increased sales and increased commissions combined with a 4 percent decrease in cost of sales.

* In the six months following implementation of my training program, turnover was reduced by 40 percent and absenteeism was reduced by 23 percent.

Sales:

Have set sales records and won sales awards in jobs selling appliances and autos.

- Set store records (total dollar value of sales) in four of five years as an appliance salesperson.

- Have won three sales awards from two appliance manufacturers, including top salesperson in Dade County and top salesperson in South Florida.

- Named best new salesperson, Kendrick Auto Sales, 1996.

Work History:

Shoreview Appliance, Miami, FL

Sales manager, Mar. 1995–present.
Hire, train, and supervise a staff of four full-time and seven part-time salespeople. Implement an ongoing training program.

Full-time salesperson, Sept. 1989–Feb. 1995.
Sold a full range of large and small appliances and was consistently the top-performing full-time salesperson.

Kendrick Auto Sales, Miami, FL

Part-time new car salesperson, Jan. 1996–present.
In my first full year, sold more new cars than any other part-time salesperson at the dealership.

Education:
Florida University, Miami, FL
Bachelor of Science in Business/Sales and Marketing, 1989

Other:
Automobile Sales Institute, Orlando, FL
Certificate, Automotive Sales Management Training Course, 1997
South Florida Auto Dealers Association, Miami, FL
Certificate, "Motivate to Sell" Seminar, 1996
English/Spanish bilingual

er-friendly because it is quicker to scan. On the other hand, most scanning these days is done by computers. Once a computer flags your resume as a result of a search, a potential employer may welcome the complete information found on a combination resume.

Use a combination resume if:

• You have a solid track record—lots of skills, achievements, and dazzling job descriptions to showcase—and are seeking a job that requires those same skills, even if in a different industry.

The Combination Resume Template

Name

Street address; city, state, ZIP; telephone; fax number; e-mail address; Web address

Objective

Summary

Skill area: name or description of skill, how you have used it, what you accomplished

Skill area: name or description of skill, how you have used it, what you accomplished

Skill area: name or description of skill, how you have used it, what you accomplished

Skill area: name or description of skill, how you have used it, what you accomplished

Experience (chronological order, from most recent to most distant)

Company name, city, and state

Job title, dates of employment

Description of duties and responsibilities

Making the Most of Weak Spots in Your Experience

Common weak spots and how to handle them:

- **Long employment gaps:** Use a functional resume, which emphasizes your skills, rather than your career track or employment dates. Explain in your cover letter the reasons for your periods of unemployment, and, if appropriate, mention what you did during those periods that was productive. For example, if you took a year off to work as a volunteer with an organization that builds homes for low-income people, by all means say so. If you were self-employed during a period of joblessness, list the self-employment on your resume as a job. (See Jonathan's resume, showing his part-time business, Brilliant Smear Designs.) You do not need to go into detail about whether the self-employment was full-time or part-time, or how much money you made. The important thing is that you did something productive with your time.

- **Frequent job changes:** Again, use a functional resume to de-emphasize dates of employment. If there are good reasons for the job changes (i.e., your company shut down or moved to another state; your job was outsourced), explain them in your cover letter. If the reasons are not so easily explainable, don't try to do so here, but be prepared to explain them in an interview. (You'll learn how to do this in chapter eight.)

- **No clear career path:** Once again, use a functional resume to focus on what has been constant: the development of skills that you have used at various jobs and can also transfer to the job you are seeking.

Accomplishment statement

Company name, city, and state

Job title, dates of employment

Description of duties and responsibilities

Accomplishment statement

Company name, city, and state

Job title, dates of employment

Description of duties and responsibilities

Accomplishment statement

Education (chronological order, from most recent to most distant)

Institution name, city, and state

Degree or certification, major field or subject area, date

Description of coursework, skills acquired, and so on if relevant

Other Information (optional; professional associations, relevant volunteer activities, languages, and so on)

Customizing Your Resume for Different Situations

If you have used your p.p.s. to figure out what job is right for you, and written the type of resume that is most likely to land you interviews for that job, you may not need to customize your resume for specific employers. Since you are taking steady aim at one target, one resume should be all you need.

If you do any customizing at all, the changes you make should be minor. As mentioned earlier, you could produce one resume with a keyword list at the top, and one without. Another example: Let's say that a specific job opening calls for a specific experience that you have but did not mention (or did not emphasize) in your resume. You could highlight the experience in your cover letter. But the cover letter may not get scanned into the employer's computer along with your resume and probably will not be searched for keywords. If the person seeking interviewees searches the computer for resumes listing the required experience, yours won't come up. In this case, it is worthwhile to add a sentence to your resume. If you have your own computer and laser printer, it's easy enough to do. If you have to pay someone to make the change, you'll invest more time and money. But the extra effort could very well get you the interview.

A note of caution: Be very careful never to send two different versions of your resume to one company, even if the recipients are not the same. Make sure that anyone who is sending your resume on your behalf is also sending a resume identical to the one you will show in an interview.

When you write your resume, do your best to include all the information that will be important to all potential employers. But when a special circumstance comes up, be prepared to go the extra mile to show that you're the right person for the job. And if you put in the time and energy to customize your resume, always get several copies of the alternate, in case a similar situation occurs.

The Cover Letter

Every resume you send out needs to be accompanied by a cover letter.

The cover letter:

CHOOSE YOUR WORDS CAREFULLY

The tone of your resume must be professional. Avoid being too familiar (don't use "I" or "you") or informal (avoid slang). On the other hand, don't use big, pretentious-sounding words like "conceptualized" and "optimized." And avoid glittering generalities—vague, overused words such as "dynamic." Say good things about yourself, but say *specific* good things. Otherwise, your resume will sound like empty bragging.

Cover Letter Template

Heading:
Your name
Address
City, State Zip
Date

Inside Address:
Recipient's name,
Recipient's title
Company name
Address
City, State Zip

Salutation:
Dear Ms./Mr./Dr. Recipient:

Body:
First paragraph: Tell what job you are applying for and how you found out about it. If you heard about the job from someone the recipient knows, use that person's name in the first sentence, to grab the reader's attention.

Second paragraph: Tell why you are the right person for the job. In a sentence or two, show that you have knowledge of the industry, company, and/or job. List any relevant qualifications that are not on your resume. Highlight two or three especially significant items that appear on your resume and direct the reader to the resume. If you are responding to an advertisement, repeat key words from the ad.

Third paragraph: (if needed): Explain any problem areas, such as long periods of unemployment.

Last paragraph: Thank the reader for her consideration. State when and how you will follow up.

Closing:
Sincerely,

Your Signature

Your Printed Name

- Is always written to a specific individual, about a specific job. It is never a form letter.

- Is always one page, no more.

- Always focuses on what you can do for the employer, not what you want.

Make sure you address your cover letter to the correct individual and spell her name and title correctly. If you don't have the name, call the company's Human Resources department, or the department you are applying to, and ask for the person's name and title. Unless you're answering a blind ad (more about these in chapter six), you have the company's name and can get the telephone number from information. Even if the job posting says "no calls," call. You're not calling to apply for the job, but merely to request the kind of information that is requested every day. And you don't have to tell the person you talk to your name, so the call can't work against you. Simply say that you are addressing a letter and want to make sure you have the person's name and title correct. If the name leaves any doubt as to whether the person is male or female, ask so that you can use the correct salutation in your letter.

If you are simply unable to find out the person's name, address your letter to the title or the department head mentioned in the job lead.

The main purpose of the cover letter is to convince the reader that your resume is worthy of serious consideration. It should make the reader so interested in you that he reads your resume immediately and takes action on it.

What do you say in a cover letter to grab a reader's interest and get him to read your resume?

- Tell why you're the right person for the job. Highlight two or three facts on your resume that are especially relevant to the job, then direct the reader to your resume for more information.

- Briefly show off your knowledge of the industry, the company, and/or the specific job.

REFERENCE SHEET TEMPLATE

References for Your Name

Reference's name
Job title
Company, city, state
Address
Phone

Reference's name
Job title
Company, city, state
Address
Phone

Reference's name
Job title
Company, city, state
Address
Phone

Reference's name
Job title
Company, city, state
Address
Phone

The cover letter is also the place to explain any problem areas in your resume, such as long periods of unemployment.

Plain block format, with all lines beginning at the left margin, is the most popular format for business letters, including cover letters. Variations are acceptable, though. For example, you may choose to center the heading, date, and closing. Of course, do not include the heading if you are using printed stationery.

Keep everything about your cover letter short: short words, short sentences, short paragraphs.

What about References?

If you have some high-profile people in the same industry rooting for you, or a reference who is well thought of by your potential employer, sending references right away along with your cover letter and resume can be a help. You may also want to use references early in the process if you are changing careers or if the job you are seeking will be somewhat dependent on your connections. As an example, a sales manager who is expected to bring clients with him to his next job may want to send some enthusiastic letters from clients early on in the decision process. Otherwise, wait to be asked. You will be sending out dozens of resumes, and you don't want your references to be overused. It's hard for a reference to be enthusiastic about you 35 times in a row! In addition, being discriminating about when references are sent may minimize the risk that your current employer will find out that you're job shopping. If you're close to an offer, this is the right time to volunteer your references if they haven't already been requested. Regardless of when they are sent, references should be listed on a separate sheet of paper. Paper and typeface must match your resume. There is no reason to include "references available on request" on your resume. This is understood.

Who Makes a Good Reference?

The term "reference" really refers to two different things: job references, and what used to be called character or personal references.

You don't have any choice about who your job references are; they're the companies you've worked for. Your potential employer will contact them based on information you list in your resume. Increasingly, companies will give out only your job title, dates of employment, and salary history. This is to avoid potential lawsuits from disgruntled ex-employees or potential employers. This can work in your favor if you've had problems at a past job. However, there is nothing to stop a company from telling your prospective employer anything he wants to know, especially if the company has your written permission to do so. If they adored you at your last job, it can be to your great advantage to get a lengthy written recommendation from them.

The less information potential employers get from your job references, the more important your character references, or personal references, are. These are the references you will list on your reference sheet. Choose them wisely. Line up at least four. That way, if one is out of town or difficult to reach at a given time, a potential employer will still be able to contact three references.

"Personal" is a bit of a misnomer here since these people will also, preferably, be individuals with whom you have a professional relationship and not just your best buddies. Always provide professional references unless you are specifically asked for a "personal" reference.

An ideal reference is:

- Someone who holds a position of greater responsibility or authority than the position you are seeking; preferably someone in the same general

field and someone your potential employer will recognize as a person of achievement and integrity.

- Someone who knows both your character and your abilities. Remember, employers are looking for the right people, not just the right skills. And your references may be their best sources of information about what kind of person you are. The longer a person has known you, and the more settings in which he has known you, the stronger he will be as a reference.

- Someone who thinks very highly of you and can communicate her enthusiasm about you and the reasons for it. If you have any doubt about whether a potential reference will say good things about you, find another reference.

- Someone who is willing to take the time to be a good reference. The person will probably have to talk on the phone to more than one potential employer, and may even be asked to write letters of recommendation. Always ask before you list a person as a reference. Let the person know each time you give her name and number to a potential employer, so she knows that she may be getting a call, and from whom.

These people might be:

- *Professional friends or mentors.* These are people who have achieved success and status in your field. They are probably older and more experienced than you are. It may be someone who worked at the same company you did, in a higher position, but who was not your boss.

- *Employers, past or present.* If you had a strong, close working relationship with an employer, it may be appropriate to use that person as a personal reference, as well as a job reference. This person will certainly know about your skills and work habits. If he also knows you as a person well enough to speak for your character, he makes a wonderful reference.

- *Professors or teachers.* If, in college, you had a special working relationship with a professor of marketing (for example, if you provided volunteer research assistance for his pet project) and are now seeking a marketing position: bingo. This person is especially valuable if you have kept in touch, so that he can speak knowledgeably about your current character.

- *Community leaders.* These people may not be in your field, but if they are well known and highly respected, they can be good references. If you have spent the past five years working with a respected community leader on a charitable project, that person's assessment of your character will probably carry considerable weight.

A bit of advice: If you have not, in the past, cultivated these kinds of relationships, now you know why you should.

Making a Good Impression

The most difficult and important part of creating a good resume is writing it right. But if you don't produce it right, your hard work may never pay off. A resume and cover letter that don't look professional and polished won't get you an interview, no matter how well written they are. And, in these technology-dependent times, a resume that can't stand up to scanning, faxing, and photocopying literally isn't worth the paper it's printed on.

If you are fortunate enough to own (or have access to) a computer and laser printer, all you need to buy is stationery. If not, you will need to go to a desktop publishing company or a printing company to produce your resume. These professionals can set up your resume according to your specifications and print as many copies as you need.

Stationery

You will need good-quality stationery that will feed easily through laser printers, photocopiers, scanners, and fax machines. Choose 8-1/2 x 11-inch, 20- to 25-pound paper that is white or cream-colored. You may choose a paper with a subtle texture (linen, for example) or watermark. Avoid colors, unusual textures, patterns, or anything that could possibly be seen as cute or unprofessional. Buy plenty of paper; you

want all your correspondence and documents to be on matching paper. That includes resumes, cover letters, reference sheets, follow-up thank-you letters, and so on. Be sure to buy matching envelopes, too.

Your paper choice will depend, in part, on your field. Attorneys and corporate executives need a formal, expensive look. No matter what position you are seeking, a clean, professional presentation never hurts. Avoid anything trendy or gimmicky at all costs.

Office supply stores and stationery stores carry a wide variety of papers that will meet your needs. You should find the information you need on the label: weight, color, texture, and technology-friendliness. If you're not sure, ask.

Printing

No matter what kind of job you're seeking, it is very unlikely that you need to have your resumes printed on an offset printing press. But you must use a laser printer, preferably a 600 dots per inch (dpi) laser printer.

Do not have your resume printed on any printer that is not a laser printer. Dot matrix, ink jet, near-letter-quality (NLQ), and thermal printers are not good enough. For one thing, your resume will look unprofessional compared to those printed on laser printers. Even more important, a resume printed with less than laser quality may not be scannable. And that, alone, could cost you a job.

More and more companies immediately scan all resumes they receive, store them on computer, and toss the paper original. If the software that reads your resume into the computer (called optical character recognition, or OCR, software) doesn't recognize every letter of your resume, it will not scan properly.

For reasons of technology and professionalism, there's only one acceptable ink color: black.

A word about photocopies: Avoid them. Get as many laser-printed copies of your resume as you will need. A photocopied document will not be quite as sharp as an original, may not scan properly, and will not fax as clearly. If you must use a photo-

Academic Resume Template

An academic resume has a slightly different form from general resumes, putting educational information first. Here is a template for an academic resume:

Your Name

Address

City, State Zip

Education:
Doctorate, field, university, date

Master's degree, field, university, date

Undergraduate degree, major, university, date

Academic Work History (teaching and administrative positions)

"Outside" Work History (any positions held outside academia)

Honors:
(fellowships, grants, and so on)

Professional Organizations

Research and Publications

copy, you must use a high-quality photocopier with a fresh toner cartridge to produce a copy that looks as much like the original as possible. And, of course, the photocopy must be on your stationery, not on generic photocopier paper.

Typeface

Your resume's typeface (also called a font) must be compatible with all the different types of technology it will encounter as it makes its rounds. It must scan easily and it should be easily readable by human eyes as well—just in case!

Choose a common text typeface such as Arial, Helvetica, New Century Schoolbook, Palatino, Times, or Times New Roman. Both OCR software and humans find these fonts easy to read. Avoid decorative typefaces and script or handwriting fonts. And stick to one typeface; don't mix fonts. Using a single font not only for your resume and cover letter but for all your documents helps to create a consistent image that employers will quickly associate with you.

Use a type size between 10 points and 14 points.

Use boldface sparingly—for headings, not whole sentences. Keep in mind that bold type can blur and be hard to read when your resume is faxed or photocopied. Italic type is hard for humans to read, and some OCR software has trouble with italics and underlining.

Do not use decorative lines (vertical or horizontal), multicolumn layouts, special effects such as shading, graphics, illustrations, and so on. OCR software reads letters, numbers, and basic punctuation, and that's about it.

Be sure to leave plenty of white space on the page. Wide margins and ample spacing between lines of type make your resume look more professional and much easier to read, for both humans and computers.

Portfolios, Demos, and Samples

For some jobs, samples of what you can do tell an employer volumes more than any resume can. If you're an illustrator, video game creator, or musician, you will need to provide samples of your work along with your resume.

The form in which samples are provided depends entirely on what you do. Just make sure that your samples are as professionally done as your resume, and that you follow industry standards. For example, will potential employers expect to keep your samples or return them to you? If they are expensive and must be returned to you, make this clear. State when you need the samples back. If possible, drop by to pick up your samples yourself; this gives you a reason to visit the employer in person. If this is not possible, provide a preaddressed, postage-paid return package (for the employer's convenience and your protection).

Of course, never send out original samples for which you do not have backup copies.

THE *Art* of NETWORKING

CHAPTER FOUR

You've probably heard of the theory called "six degrees of separation." It's the idea that every person on earth is separated from every other person by six people or fewer.

The term "degree" refers to how close the relationship is. A person you know (say, your best friend) is in your first degree, a person that person knows (your best friend's college roommate) is in your second degree, and so on. According to the theory, absolutely everybody is in your sixth degree, via one path of degrees or another.

So, if the theory is correct, your worst-case scenario is: You know somebody who knows somebody who knows somebody who knows somebody who knows somebody who knows the person who can hire you to do the job you want to do! (And the theory just may be correct, more or less. It was developed by Guglielmo Marconi, inventor of the telegraph, and is based on sound statistical logic.)

The process by which you navigate the degrees and close the gap between you and

your future employer is called networking. Since "networking" is one of those words that people sometimes use when they really mean "hanging out," it may be necessary to say this: Networking does not mean hanging out at the nearest bar, coffee shop, or mall until someone walks up to you and offers you a job. Very simply, networking means letting people know what you want, and asking them if they can help you get it.

Get Ready to Network

Getting ready to network is a fairly simple three-step process:

- Step One: Make a master list of your current network.

- Step Two: Create a system to keep track of your networking contacts.

- Step Three: Prioritize your list and set goals.

Step One

Start by making a list of all the people you want to include in your network. Go through your Rolodex (or wherever you keep your address and telephone directory) and put on the list everybody who might conceivably know anybody who might know somebody. (You get the idea—don't rule anybody out.) Definitely include all your relatives and friends; neighbors; acquaintances you know through hobbies, community activities, and so on; people you do business with (your doctor, dentist, veterinarian, lawyer, accountant, insurance agent, and so on); and anybody else you can think of. If you're still in touch with fellow students or professors from your college days, include them, too.

The only question mark is whether to include people you work with. If you don't want your current employer to know you're job-hunting, obviously don't let any coworkers know you're looking. If your employer knows you're looking elsewhere, by all means include your coworkers in your network.

Step Two

Once you've created your master list for networking, and before you pick up the phone, create a system to keep track of your contacts. This could be a looseleaf notebook with one page for each contact, or a four- by six-inch file box with a card for each contact.

Step Three

Finally, prioritize your list and set goals. Your first contacts should be the people you think are most likely to be able to help you. You may want to rank each person on your list as a "1," meaning call now; a "2," meaning second priority; and so on. Set a goal to make a given number of contacts each week (40 to 50 is a reasonable number), then divide the number over the four to six days a week that you will actively network.

The First Degree: How to Approach Your Network

Before making a contact, think about what your relationship is with the person you are calling, what you know about her, and what she might be able to do for you. Think through how you want to focus the conversation. Don't expect the person on the other end of the phone to figure out what it is you want from her. Give her specific information about your goal and be prepared to ask specific questions. ("Do you know anyone who does this job, or is in this industry?") Always ask if this is a good time to talk, and ask about the other person before launching into your requests.

Because the purpose of every networking contact is to let the person know what you want and ask for help in getting it, your p.p.s. will play a starring role in your networking calls. By sharing your p.p.s., you give your contacts a brief, clear statement of who you are and what you can do for an employer. You can then talk specifically about what you'd like the person to do for you.

Sample Contact Sheet

Name of person contacted:

_____

Address: _____

Telephone: _____

Learned about this person from:_____

Information about this person:

(This could be the person's job title and company or any other information you want to remember.)

_____

_____

Contact record:

Date: _____

Action:
(Left a message, talked to the person, sent a note?)

_____

_____

This person referred me to these people: *

_____

_____

_____

_____

* Of course, you will make contact sheets for these people, too.

Family and Friends

There are three reasons why your family and friends are good people to begin with when you're networking.

- First, you can usually count on them to take time to talk with you and to help you in any way they can.

- Second, you're not likely to be intimidated by them. Practice telling them about your p.p.s. and asking them for help. By the time you get around to calling mere acquaintances and strangers, you'll be a veteran networker.

- Third, the people they refer you to are likely to want to help you because of your close relationship with the relative or friend who makes the connection. Wouldn't you be more willing to help your brother's best friend than your coworker's brother-in-law's personal trainer?

Obviously, your networking contacts with friends and family will be more informal than those with people you barely know. Still, be sensitive to the other person's schedule and needs.

Your conversations with these people often will be longer than those with people you don't know well. Let them know how much thought you have put into creating your p.p.s. and defining your job goal, and how enthusiastic you are about reaching it. Ask open-ended questions like, "If you were in my position, what would you do? How would you go about finding this job?" Sometimes an outsider—someone with a perspective quite different from yours—will come up with a totally unexpected but brilliant idea. If the person doesn't really understand the job you want to do, or the industry you're in, take the time to explain. It's possible that he knows someone you need to know but doesn't realize it. Ten minutes into your explanation of exactly what a systems team leader does, your cousin Jerry may hear you say "M.I.S." and say, "Oh, okay, M.I.S. The guy who lives across the street from me is a V.P. of M.I.S." Home run.

Neighbors and Other Social Acquaintances

Networking with neighbors and acquaintances can be very informal. You may run into your neighbors while walking your dog, working in your yard, or getting your mail. If you belong to a community or religious organization, approach the people you know there in person or on the phone. Ask if they have a minute, then keep it brief. Again, your p.p.s. is a terrific way to quickly communicate who you are and what you can do for employers. Explain what job you're looking for and ask if the person knows anyone in your industry or knows of any job openings. Always have a pen and notepad on hand to write down names and telephone numbers. Hand the person your resume and ask if he would mind holding onto it, in case he meets someone who might be interested. (Try to have a few copies of your resume with you all the time. But if you get caught without one, ask if you can drop one by later. This gives you an opportunity to remind the person of your job search.) And always end by thanking the person for his time and help.

People You Do Business With

Your doctor, dentist, veterinarian, lawyer, accountant, insurance agent, and all the other people you do business with are excellent networking contacts. For one thing, you are their customer. They should be willing to take a few minutes to listen and to help you if they can. For another thing, these are people who know a lot of people. If they're successful, they probably understand the importance of networking and do it well themselves.

These are also very busy people. Try to approach them at a relaxed time. (Don't call your tax accountant on April 14 to talk about your job search.) If there's any chance they won't know immediately who you are, make the connection for them. ("Dr. Greenley, this is Patricia Patterson. I'm the one with the two harlequin Great Danes, Merlin and Matilda.") Ask if they have a few minutes, or if there's a time when you can call back. State briefly why you are calling. Ask if they know anyone in your field. Whether they do or not, thank them for their time.

The Second Degree and Beyond: Calling People You Don't Know

As you begin working your way through your list of first-degree contacts, it won't be long before you get the names of some promising second-degree contacts. This is where many people spend a lot of time sitting by the phone with sweaty palms, wishing they would win the lottery and not have to call someone they don't know and ask for help. If you are a born people person or have years of experience in sales, you're probably immune to sweaty-palms syndrome. If not:

- Remember that most people actually like to be asked for information. In a very real sense, your call is a compliment. It is a way of saying, "You're someone who's plugged in. You have information and contacts that I need to know." Approach people with this attitude that they have something of value that you hope they will share with you.

- Say the name of the person who referred you in your very first sentence. ("Ms. Yoshino, this is Carla Gooden, Cheryl Gooden's sister. Cheryl suggested that I call you....") This gives the person you are calling a context for the call and a connection to you.

- Ask if you are calling at a good time and, if so, assure the person that you need only a few minutes of her time.

- Share your p.p.s. and then be specific about what job you want and what you'd like the person to do for you. If you have been told that Ms. Yoshino knows someone in your field, you may want her to give you the person's name and phone number. Or you may want Ms. Yoshino to give your resume to her contact, or to introduce the two of you. Listen carefully to what Ms. Yoshino says and to her tone of voice and level of enthusiasm. She may offer to make an introduction for you without being asked. If she doesn't, try to get a sense of whether she would be willing to do so.

- As you bring the call to a close, consider asking the person if you can send her your resume (if this hasn't already come up). Also, ask if you can

give her your telephone number, in case you can return the favor some day. (This also ensures that she will have your number if she happens to meet the person who can hire you at a dinner party that evening.) And, of course, thank her for her time and for any information she has given you.

• Yes, there are exceptions to every rule. A few people you approach will not be willing to help you. Some will not even make a pretense of being polite. When that happens, don't take it personally. After all, this person doesn't even know you, so he can't be singling you out for bad treatment. Either he's having a bad day or he's just not a nice person. Give him the benefit of the doubt and don't sink to his level. Apologize for disturbing him (even though you know he was disturbed before he ever heard your name), and move on to your next call. You never know what the future may bring. He may call you the next day, explain that you phoned right after he found out he was being audited, and give you the lead you need.

Follow Up

Follow up most of your networking calls with a written thank-you. (You can make exceptions for your immediate family, but not many others.) Not only is this polite, but your note will be an added reminder of you and your job goal. The person will think of you again and, maybe, think of a connection that slipped her mind when you talked. If you think it's appropriate (or if you suggested it when you talked), include a copy of your resume. Mention any contacts the person offered that you have followed up on. ("I talked with your friend Alberto Ruiz, and he was as helpful as you said he would be. Thanks again for suggesting that I call him.")

When someone gives you information that leads to a great contact, a job interview, or a job, be sure to let that person know how much she helped, and say thank you again.

The Informational Interview

When your networking efforts lead you to a person who knows your industry inside and out and has contacts galore, try to set up an informational interview. Unlike a job interview, this is a meeting at which you'll ask most of the questions.

There are several reasons to ask for an in-person meeting with an especially good contact. For starters, you're more likely to get the person's undivided attention for a period of time. Also, an in-person meeting will establish a closer connection between you and your contact. He'll be more likely to remember you and more motivated to help you—assuming you make a good impression. Finally, meeting you in person gives your contact an opportunity to size up your appearance and presentation. He is much more likely to refer you to other people he knows if he sees that you dress and act like a professional.

Here's how to prepare for, arrange, and conduct an informational interview:

1. When you're on the phone with someone who you realize is a gold mine of information, consider whether to ask for an informational interview on the spot. If the person is enthusiastic and helpful on the phone, answering your questions in detail and offering help you haven't even asked for, chances are he will be happy to meet with you. If your contact is less forthcoming, you may need to be patient. After the call, send a thank-you note and follow up on any leads the person gave you. Wait a couple of weeks, then call to ask for a brief meeting.

2. Offer to meet wherever and whenever is most convenient for your contact. His office is usually the best place, but he may prefer to meet elsewhere. Offer to take him to lunch if that fits his schedule better. Ask how much time he has for you, and promise to limit your meeting to that time frame.

3. Prepare specific, intelligent questions that you can reasonably expect the person to answer. You should already be well informed about the industry in general and be able to talk knowledgeably about it. Your questions for your contact should be those that only an insider can answer: Is there anything you can do that you haven't already done to prepare yourself for the job you want? Does he know of particular companies, departments, or managers that you should target? And so on. Make sure to bring at least one copy of your resume, and business cards if you have them.

4. Dress appropriately. If you're meeting at the contact's office, dress as you would for a job interview. But if he asks you to meet him at his country club after his golf game, office dress will seem out of place and may even make him uncomfortable.

5. Ask if you can take notes. (Your contact may share information that he doesn't want passed on. If he asks you to keep something confidential, don't write it down and don't pass it on.) During the conversation, as he mentions people or companies you'd like to follow up with, jot down their names. Then, at the end of the meeting, ask him if he would mind your contacting these people and using his name.

6. Keep the meeting to the agreed-upon time frame and thank the person for his time and expertise. If your resume hasn't already been discussed, ask the person if you can leave a copy of it with him. Tell him you would be happy to hear from him if there is some way you can repay his kindness. Follow up with a thank-you note within a day or two after the meeting.

Taking Advantage of Ready-Made Networks

In addition to expanding your personal network, you will want to make use of various professional, academic, and social networks. You may choose to join a few organizations (alumni clubs, trade and professional associations, or community groups), to become more active in groups you already belong to, or to attend career-oriented and social events where you are likely to make good contacts.

What networks you choose to use will depend on your job goal. Think about where you are likely to meet the most people who can help you. Ask other people in your industry where they network.

Meetings, Parties, and the Rest: How to Work a Room

Working a room—meeting and greeting people you don't know, making conversation, asking for and sharing information—is a skill. The more you practice it, the better (and more comfortable) you'll be at it. And once you learn, you can apply the skill anyplace there are people, from a wedding reception to an office party to a trade show.

Before you go, prepare.

- *Know what you're getting into.* Learn as much as you can about the person or organization sponsoring the event, and about the event itself. Your personal network should be helpful in leading you to people who can clue you in. Or simply call the organization's office and question the person who answers the phone. Find out whether the event is primarily social or primarily business. This will guide you in how you approach people and how directly you talk about your job search. Try to find out who will be there. Make sure you know how to dress. There's nothing worse than walking into a room full of strangers and watching all eyes turn toward you because you're obviously overdressed or underdressed.

- *Know your purpose.* Once you know all about the event, decide what

your purpose is in going. Do you want a chance to meet new people in your industry and listen to what they have to say about various companies? Do you hope to get some concrete job leads? Make sure your purpose is reasonable, given what you know about the event.

- *Know what you're going to say.* Some very misguided experts actually recommend that you write and practice a word-for-word script of how you'll introduce yourself, hilarious stories you'll tell, and so on. We think not. In the first place, very few people can do this without sounding stilted. In the second place, regurgitating memorized lines is no substitute for genuine conversation. You want to make connections, not speeches. But you will be more at ease, and a better networker, if you go with some ideas about how you'll handle these situations:

  1. Introducing yourself. This can be especially intimidating if you're unemployed, since people often identify themselves by their company and/or their job. ("Hi, I'm Jordan. I'm a junior partner with Smith, Smith, and Smith.") Decide ahead of time how you're going to identify yourself. Think about what you have in common with the other people who will be attending, and also about how up front you want to be about the fact that you're job-hunting. If everybody in the room will be an interior designer and it's a business event where you want to do some serious networking, you might try: "Hi, I'm Lisa Baron. I was with Malone Studio for the past five years." On the other hand, if you're headed for a social event that will be attended by people with all kinds of careers, you might just start with, "Hi, my name is Lisa Baron. I'm an interior designer."

  2. Answering the inevitable questions. "What do you do?" and "Where do you work?" If you don't answer these questions in your introduction, they are likely to be asked soon after. Once you've provided a brief description of your industry or expertise, you can mention your last job and then state briefly what you're looking for. (Remember your p.p.s.!) If you are asked why you left your last job, take the question in stride. Explain in brief, matter-of-fact terms how your former

company was reorganized and your postition changed, or how a change in management caused some personnel shifts—whatever. Just be sure to plan for the question, in case it gets asked, and be prepared with a reasoned and confident answer.

3. Starting a conversation. The easiest ways to do this are to ask a non-threatening question ("How long have you been a member?") or comment on something in the room ("Isn't that a beautiful tapestry? I wonder where it was made."). You can put people at ease by telling them about something funny that happened to you. Don't give anybody any information that could come back to haunt you. ("She told me she got falling-down drunk at the Christmas party, bumped into her boss's husband in the coat closet, and kissed him on the lips!") But a willingness to acknowledge your imperfections and an ability to make people laugh are two traits that will make people like you and remember you.

4. Consider taking a partner. The idea here is not to have someone to cling to all evening. The idea is to double your efforts. If you know someone else who is going to the same event, go together. Keep your partner's interests in mind as you talk to people, and make sure she does the same for you. Agree in advance that at a certain point in time, you'll find each other and introduce each other to the contacts you've made.

5. Make sure you're prepared with plenty of business cards, copies of your resume, and a pen and notepad. (If it's a social function, leave your briefcase and resumes in your car. If you want to give one to someone, you can walk outside with him as he leaves, and not risk bringing too much business to the party.)

Once you're there:

- *Wear a pleasant expression, not a plastic smile or a mask of fear.*

- *Forget about whatever discomfort you're feeling; focus on other people.*

When you approach people, remind yourself that they're human beings with problems and fears a lot like yours. Ask people about themselves (nothing personal, of course), and listen when they answer. Listen for opportunities to share information; you're here to give, as well as to get. Look at the person you're talking to, not over her shoulder to see who you can approach next. A genuine interest in other people can't be faked, and can't be overestimated.

- *Look for other people who are alone.* They're easy to approach and will be grateful to have someone to talk to. Just introduce yourself and ask one of those nonthreatening questions.

- *Don't be intimidated by groups.* If you see a group of people that looks interesting, or overhear a conversation that interests you, join in. Simply stand on the edge of the group, make eye contact with the person who's speaking, and respond to what's being said by nodding or smiling. When there's a lull in the conversation, some savvy person in the group will probably acknowledge you and give you a chance to introduce yourself. If not, say something like, "I hope I'm not intruding, but I am interested in what you are saying."

Networking is a valuable skill that takes some practice. But after you've made a few connections, it's likely you'll never let another opportunity to sell yourself slip by.

THE GREAT
Online
job
HUNT

*You can't say
you've covered
all the bases in
your job hunt
until you've
taken your job
hunt **online.**
The information
superhighway is
a two-way
cyberstreet. You
need to gather
information, and
you also need to
get the word out
about **who you
are** and **what
you can do.***

This chapter is divided into two main sections: first, how to use the Internet to get information about careers, industries, and job openings; and second, how to use the Internet to let employers know about you.

Part One: Using the Internet to Get Information

Career and job-hunting resources on the Internet fall into several broad categories. There are career centers, megasites where you'll find a smorgasbord of career information and services. There are job databases, basically the electronic version of help-

If You're Not Online Yet...

 If you have a computer but it's not yet linked to the Internet, you need two things: Internet connection software, and an Internet Service Provider. (If you have an older computer that doesn't have a modem, you'll need one of those, too.)

You can find an Internet Service Provider by looking under that heading in the Yellow Pages. Or ask your friends who are online what service provider they use. Some popular providers you may have heard of are America Online and AT&T. There are also many widely available books that can help you get started, like Point and Click Jobfinder (also by Seth Godin, Dearborn Financial Publishing, 1996), which comes with a disk to get you onto America Online. Prices and services offered vary from provider to provider, so call a few service providers for information before you sign up with one. When you are ready to sign up, your service provider can tell you everything you need to know to get started, including what Internet connection software you need and where to get it. You'll need to provide some basic information about your computer, such as the brand name, model, and amount of memory; and some information about your modem. Some service providers give you the software free when you sign up.

One note of caution: If you are currently employed and don't necessarily want your employer to know that you are looking, using your computer at work for your search is probably not a great idea. If you do choose to look while at work (on your lunch hour or coffee break, of course) be discreet. You don't want to run the risk of your employer stumbling on an e-mail exchange with a potential new employer or a voice-mail message confirming an interview. If you don't have a computer, you may be able to access the Internet at a nearby public library, university, school, or copy shop, such as Kinko's. Just call and ask.

Web Sites about Jobs

If you know anything about the vastness of the Web, you won't be surprised to know that not only are there tens of thousands of sites about jobs, there are also Web sites that list Web sites about jobs. None of these lists will include every single Web site that has to do with jobs and careers. Some list hundreds of job-related sites, while others list thousands. All are organized differently and have different strengths and weaknesses. So it's worthwhile to take a look at several of them.

The Definitive Guide to Internet Career Resources
http://phoenix.placement.oakland.edu/career/Guide.htm
A relatively small list (hundreds, not thousands) of high-quality sites, listed alphabetically.

A Handy Guide
http://www.ahandyguide.com/cat1/employ.htm
Online career information organized into more than 10,000 categories.

JobHunt
http://www.job-hunt.org
A listing of useful Internet-accessible job-search resources and services.

Best Bets from the Net
http://www.lib.umich.edu/chdocs/employment
A relatively small, high-quality list courtesy of the University of Michigan.

Job Seekers
http://www.helpwantedpage.com/gtr/Website1_19/New/
rec.resources/RecuitRes.html
Yes, its URL is a pain. But this is a long, long list (thousands, not hundreds) of sites.

Nerd World Media:Jobs and Related Links
http://www.nerdworld.com/users/dstein/nw102.html
This list's special feature is that it provides capsule descriptions of sites listed, making it easier to find the sites that interest you. Sites are organized both alphabetically and by category.

wanted ads, where you can go to find job openings. There are Web sites where you can research industries, and there are company Web sites, where you can learn all about specific employers (often including what jobs they have available). Finally, there are online versions of books, magazines, and other career resources.

By the time you read this, there may well be 50,000 Web sites for job hunters. This chapter tells you about a few of the biggest and best and how to find the ones that have what you're looking for.

Career Centers

Career centers are supermarkets of information for job seekers. They offer a broad array of information and services, often including databases of both job openings and resumes; lots of information about jobs and careers, from how to write a resume to information about salaries and companies; and listings of products and services for sale.

Here are a few of the best-known career centers.

AOL Workplace

(For America Online subscribers only.) Navigate to the AOL Workplace by typing in the keyword "jobs" or "Find a Job." This sprawling career resource has everything:

CAREERMagazine, a resume database (called The Talent Bank), job listings, resume advice, and much more. You can even schedule one-on-one career counseling or join regularly scheduled counseling sessions.

Career City

(http://www.careercity.com) Search through 125,000 jobs available by job title, company name, location, or other variables. Access information about thousands of companies.

Career Mosaic

(http://www.careermosaic.com) A big site that has pretty much everything. You can post your resume and search the job databank free of charge. Other features are special sections for first-time job seekers, for those seeking jobs in health care, and for those interested in employment overseas.

Career Path.com

(http://www.careerpath.com) More than 30 newspapers (mostly big-city dailies) have gotten together to list their help-wanted classified ads on this site. You'll find more than 200,000 job openings. Search by newspaper and type of job. There's also a resume database. It's free.

Career Resource Center

(http://www.careers.org/index.html) One of the biggest and best, it's got everything a job seeker could want.

Career Shop

(http://www.tenkey.com/cshop) This site offers a job database and a resume database, and both are free. You'll also find job fairs listed by city.

Career Web

(http://www.cweb.com) An award-winning site that has it all, including a special focus on health care, high-tech, international, and seasonal jobs.

Curry Business Systems, Inc.

(http://www. curryinc.com) This site offers an interesting monthly e-mailed newsletter on staffing and interviewing issues. They also offer an online training course for employment interviews.

e-span

(http://www.espan.com) This site has a couple of special features in addition to the basics. One is that it allows you to quickly narrow your job search to jobs that match your education, experience, other qualifications, and location. This saves a lot of time wading through "matches" that actually match only one or two facets of your dream job. Special feature number two is a salary calculator that compares the cost of living in hundreds of U.S. and international cities.

The Internet's Online Career Center

(http://www.occ.com) Another huge career center with lots of information, both job and resume databases, and links to other career-related sites, including employer Web sites. It also hosts employer open houses.

JobCenter

(http://www.jobcenter.com) In addition to all the expected resources, the resume bank here offers a special feature. When you post your resume (there is a fee for this service), it is automatically matched with job openings in the center's database. The center e-mails you the matching job description and e-mails your resume to the employer.

JobWeb

(http://www.jobweb.com) Sponsored by the National Association of Colleges and Employers. Especially good for college students and recent grads, and for job seekers looking for employment in schools.

Manpower Technical

(http://www.manpower.com) Manpower Technical collects, scans, and stores resumes in their TechBase which enables them to accurately match qualified technical professionals with the staffing needs of many Fortune 500 companies.

Microsoft Corporation

(http://www.microsoft.com/jobs) The latest version of Microsoft's Internet Explorer (version 4.0) offers astonishing tools for professional researchers. You can search the Web to locate job candidates or collect information about potential employers.

The Monster Board

(http://www.monster.com) The name says it all: lots and lots of job listings, in addition to the regular career center offerings. Special feature: relocation information and services.

Your Personal Network

(http://www.ypn.com/topics/881.html) Classified ads list jobs by category (academia to zookeepers). Plus there's a bookstore, reviews of other Web sites, and more.

MEMBERS-ONLY WEB SITES

Your Internet Service Provider (ISP) may provide its own career center, career-oriented chat groups, business reference library, or other services for subscribers only. Examples include the America Online Career Center and eWorld's eWorld of Work. Ask your ISP what career resources it offers its subscribers.

Job Databases

Job databases, also called job banks, have a narrower focus than career centers. They are the classified ads of the Internet. In fact, some are sponsored by newspapers. Others are sponsored by associations and other industry groups. Some job databases act as matchmakers, gathering information from applicants and employers and letting both sides know when there's a match. Other databases leave it to you to search the job listings.

Read online job listings the same way you read classified ads: with a wary eye. Most job databases try to weed out obvious scams like pyramid schemes, and the vast majority of listings are for valid opportunities. But there are bound to be a few rotten apples in these huge electronic baskets. If you run across one, be sure to let the database manager know about it.

Academe This Week

(http://www.chronicle.merit.edu) Sponsored by the Chronicle of Higher Education, this free site lists more than 1,000 jobs for teachers, professors, and administrators of higher education.

America's Employers

(http://www.americasemployers.com) Jobs are listed by about 40,000 employers (including biggies like Microsoft and AT&T), and you can search them for free after filling out a profile that a computer uses to match you to appropriate openings. There's also a resume bank, which is listed under "Resume Databases" later in this chapter.

America's Job Bank

(http://www.ajb.dni.us) This site, put together by the government's public Employment Service, is the online database of job openings listed at state employment offices all over the United States. To respond to a listing, you send your resume to the Employment Service, which in turn contacts the employer. You can also access

the *Occupational Outlook Handbook*, published by the Bureau of Labor Statistics. It's all free.

The Business Job Finder

(http://www.cob.ohio-state.edu/dept/fin/osujobs.htm) Just what it says—listings of jobs available in business—and then some, including company profiles and career-planning information. No charge. Also, links to career-related sites.

NAPA's Career Search

(http://www.careers.com) This site contains thousands of jobs at both the entry and professional levels—broken down by industry and field.

Exec.U.Net

(http://www.execunet.com) A members-only site with relatively hefty fees and job listings of management and executive jobs paying more than $75,000 a year.

FedWorld

(http://www.fedworld.gov) If you want to work for Uncle Sam, this is the place to search his Federal Job Announcement database. Paid for by your tax dollars.

career.com

(http://www.career.com) The focus here is on high-tech jobs. At online job fairs called CyberFairs you can "meet" potential employers.

JOBTRAK

(http://www.jobtrak.com) This site is for college students and graduates only; you'll need a password from your school to use the site. (How-to instructions are at the site.) The scholars-only requirement is a draw for employers; thousands of new jobs are listed every day. No charge to job seekers.

Salary Surveys

When you're job-hunting, it's a good idea to know what the job you want pays. Ideally, you want to know what the average is, which companies pay above average, and which companies pay below average.

Do keep in mind, though, that salary isn't the only factor in compensation. Benefits (insurance, vacations, employer-paid education, and so on) and "perks" (company car, corporate meetings in exotic locations) add to or detract from the overall compensation package.

The Internet is a good place to find salary surveys. Here are some starting places:

- JobSmart (a career center for California job hunters) has links to more than 150 salary surveys. Go to http://jobs-mart.org/tools/salary/index.htm.

- e-span (http://www.espan.com) and Career Shop (http://www.tenkey.com/cshop) both have salary surveys.

MedSearch Healthcare Careers

(http://www.medsearch.com) As you might expect, MedSearch is for job seekers in the health care industry. This is both a job database and a resume bank, and it's free.

Yahoo! Classifieds

(http://www.classifieds.yahoo.com/employment.html) Just what it says: electronic classifieds listed by city and state.

Company Web Sites (They Post Jobs, You Know)

Most companies have their own Web sites by now, and there are lots of reasons for you to check them out. For one thing, not all companies list their job openings on job databases. You may find openings listed on company Web sites that you'll find nowhere else. Also, you can learn a lot about a company by taking a close look at its Web site, from how the company is organized to what products and services it sells. Of course, exactly what information you find will depend on the individual Web site. Some companies' sites are very basic, offering just bare-bones information. Other companies' Web sites are encyclopedic, telling you everything you could possibly want to know about the company. In either case, you're likely to find an e-mail address that you can use to request an annual report or other information.

There are several fast ways to find a company's Web site. You can use a search engine (such as Yahoo!, AltaVista, or Excite) to search the Web, using the company's name as your keyword. Or you can try typing "www.thecompanysname.com" in the address field of your Web browser. You can also do a more global search by typing in a string of keywords. For example, try "electrical engineers San Francisco jobs" and just see what comes up. In addition to possibly finding the company you are looking for, you may find some other companies whose names you didn't know. Perhaps the easiest way to find a particular company's Web site is to call its main phone number and ask the telephone receptionist for the company's URL.

Researching Your Industry

To get a handle on your industry as a whole, try these methods:

- Find out the name of the most important associations in your industry and check out their Web sites. For example, if you're a business consultant—or hope to be—search the Web for the Association of Management Consulting Firms and the Council of Consulting Organizations.

- If you don't know what associations represent your industry, ask someone who works in the industry, check out industry trade publications at the library or online (often these publications are sponsored by associations), or scan the associations listed at http://www.yahoo.com/Business_and_ Economy/Organizations.

Online Publications

Many career-oriented magazines and books have online versions. To find one, use its name as your keyword and search the Web. Here are a few of the most popular online publications:

Occupational Outlook Handbook
http://www.bls.gov/ocohome.htm
This government publication is a gold mine of solid facts, figures, and forecasts about careers and jobs.

What Color Is Your Parachute: Job Hunting Online
http://www.washingtonpost.com/parachute
The online version of this longtime bestseller has tons of good material plus links to the best job-related sites on the Web.

CAREERMagazine
http://www.careermag.com
This popular magazine is a comprehensive resource for the online job seeker.

JobWeb
http://www.jobweb.com
Most material is geared for recent college graduates.

Newsgroups: Talk about Jobs!

 Newsgroups are the interchanges of the information superhighway. They're the place where you can gather information and post information at the same time. Also called Internet Discussion Groups (IDGs), newsgroups are for networking. A newsgroup is like a big room full of people who are all interested in talking about the same thing.

Some newsgroups are very general; one called misc.jobs.misc offers discussion of anything and everything that has to do with jobs. There are also newsgroups that specialize in various geographic areas and in specific industries. And there are newsgroups where employers list jobs (for example, misc.jobs.offered) and others where job seekers post resumes (misc.jobs.resumes).

Here are some places to learn more about job-related newsgroups:

- Deja News (http://www.dejanews.com/home_ps.shtml) is a place where you can learn about all the different newsgroups on the Net, search archives of past discussions, and join in current ones. Go to http://www.dejanews.com/categories/jobs.shtml to browse a list of job-related newsgroups.

- Yahoo! Jobs Newsgroups (http://www.yahoo.com/Business_and_Economy/Employment/Jobs/Usenet) lists job-related newsgroups.

- Jobline Database, a feature of CAREERMagazine (http://www.careermag.com) has archives of job-related newsgroups' discussions.

- Usenet Job Search, part of Career Mosaic (http://www.career-mosaic.com), is an index of job-related newsgroups. When you find a newsgroup that fits your interests, read through some of the archives to get a feel for the discussions. You'll find out fairly quickly if it's worth your while to check in regularly.

- Browse the Web sites of the biggest and best companies in the industry to get the big picture.

- Use business reference sites to find articles and other information about the industry. Commercepark (http://www.commercepark.com) offers a research library plus business listings and links in categories including retail, industrial, global, and nonprofit.

Search Tips: Where Do You Start?

The big question, of course, is how you wade through all of this information. Here's a strategy:

- Start by browsing through several of the Web sites about jobs and career centers listed in this chapter. Make notes about sites and features that you want to go back to or explore further. Look for job listings that seem to have lots of opportunities in your industry. Use the "bookmark" or "favorites" feature of your Web browser to record the addresses of Web sites you'll want to visit again.

- Next check out the job databases. Again, look for sites that seem geared to your industry. Do trial searches to see how easy it is to get a list of job openings that are a good match for you. (Most databases have search tips that tell you how to find what you're looking for. Take the time to read them.) The more variables you can search by, the closer the matches will be.

- When you explore a job database, find out when listings are updated. Most are updated daily or weekly. Make a note on your planning calendar to check each database as soon as it is updated. If you find a job that interests you, you want to be among the first to respond.

- When you find a job that you're interested in, go to the company's Web site to learn all you can about the employer before you send off a resume.

- Search the Web sites of companies you like, to see what jobs are listed there.

Part Two: Using the Internet to Let Employers Know about You

There are two ways to use the Internet to let employers know about you. The first is to post your resume at resume databases where employers search for job candidates. The second is to create your own Web site. Before you embark down either of these paths, a word of caution: If you are currently employed and don't want your employer to find out you're looking for a new job, the risk is high that your privacy will be violated on the Internet. You have no way of limiting access to what you post or of effectively knowing who has seen your resume or Web site. If you are not employed, or your employer knows you are job shopping, or you just aren't as paranoid as we are, by all means, read on!

Resume Databases

The flip side of a job database, a resume database is where employers come to look for you. Many allow you to post your resume for free. Some resume databases charge a fee.

It's important to know that computers, not humans, search resume banks to match resumes to employers' needs. Computers search for keywords that fit the job title; your online resume must include the proper keywords in order for the computer to recognize you as a match. (See "What Employers Want to See," chapter three on page 58.) Some services have you fill out their own form, rather than sending in your resume. The form may have a list of keywords for you to

WHY EMPLOYERS LOVE THE INTERNET

Business is booming. Unemployment is low. That means employers are eagerly seeking good, qualified employees. And most employers have discovered by now that the Internet is a good place to find them.

- It allows employers to find the people they want, no matter where in the world they are.

- It allows for fast, focused searches of huge numbers of resumes.

- Job seekers they find on the Internet have a certain amount of technology savvy, or they wouldn't be there.

How to Create Your Own Web Site

There are plenty of companies, large and small, that will create and produce a Web site for you. A Yahoo search using the keywords "Web site design" returned 1,564 sites, from Alpha Web Design (http://www.tissunique.com/alpha) to The Web Experts (http://www.isd.net/twexper1). Fees vary widely.

As always, be a smart consumer and check out companies thoroughly before giving them your business. You can also create your own Web site, and it's easier than you might imagine. You can learn how to create a Web site at webreference.com (http://www.webreference.com).

This is an "A to Z" site, with everything you need to know to create and promote a Web site. The site's "announcing" section (http://www.webreference.com/announcing.html) has links to many sites where you can list your Web site with search engines. There are also tons of books available that will help you create a professional-looking Web site. Two good ones are *How to Set up and Maintain a Web Site,* by Lincoln D. Stein (Addison-Wesley Pub. Co., 1997) and *Web Sites that Work,* by Roger Black (Hayden Books, 1997). Here are some things to keep in mind, whether you design your Web site yourself or hire someone to do it:

• Keep the design as simple as possible so that your site loads quickly. When someone shows enough interest to access your site, you don't want to keep them waiting.

• Keep it strictly professional. Don't include pages about your private life, hobbies, and so on.

• Include your resume, and make sure it's downloadable.

• On the other hand, you may want to copyright some of the material on your Web site and prevent downloading. According to current law, your work will be automatically protected to a certain extent, but better safe than sorry. This is especially true of samples of creative work, such as writing or drawings. Find out more about the copyright aspect of Web publishing at the self-publishing sites just listed, or from your Web site design firm. It never hurts to add a copyright line to your page.

- Register your Web site with Yahoo, Excite, and other major search engines, to make it easier to find. You can do this at individual search engines, or use a registration service (for a fee). Check webreference (see above) for information about how to register your site. One caveat, though. Although people have gotten job offers by establishing these links, the likelihood that an employer who is looking for someone with your exact skills will find your link on these large search engines is very, very small. There are just too many thousands of sites in competition with you.

- Try to have your site linked to major Web sites in your industry. For example, if you are a graphic designer, try to have your site listed as a link on the sites of any professional organizations you belong to. Contact the organization to find out what its policies are on linking.

choose from. Another advantage of submitting your information this way is that employers get exactly the same information, in the same form, about all applicants, making comparison easy.

One caveat about putting your resume on the Internet for all the world to see: All the world can see it. Nothing in your resume will be private anymore, including your home address and phone number. It's perfectly legal for people to go through resume banks to collect phone numbers to be used in telemarketing. Consider leaving off your address and telephone number and including only your e-mail address. For similar reasons, you may want to remove the name of your current employer (if you have one), replacing it with a generic description such as "a California-based pharmaceutical company." Before you hit the send button, read your resume closely and take out anything you don't want in the public domain.

E-mail Etiquette

E-mail is the online way to reach out and touch someone. A few reminders to ensure that you make a good e-impression:

- People don't like junk e-mail any more than they like junk mail. Make sure your e-mail messages respect the other person's time and privacy. Don't clutter up anyone's e-mailbox with unwanted or unnecessary messages.

- Keep your messages brief and to the point. Label each message with a subject line that will tell the recipient at a glance what the message is about.

- Check and double-check the spelling, grammar, and punctuation of your e-mail messages. If you—like many people—tend to miss errors when you proofread on your monitor, print out your messages before you send them, and proof them on paper.

- Check your messages for clarity and tone. Remember that the person reading your e-mail has only your words to go by; he can't see your facial expression or hear the tone of your voice. As a result, something you mean as a joke may seem like an insult to the reader. Make sure that your words convey exactly what you mean to say, and that your attitude is clear.

A+ On-line Resumes

(http://www.ol-resume.com) More than a resume bank, this is a new kind of resume service. For a fee, the company puts your resume into its database (which is advertised at various sites on the Internet) and provides you with your own Web site.

America's Employers Resume Bank

(http://www.americasemployers.com/resume.html) Part of the same site as the America's Employers job bank. There's also a career chat.

Intellimatch On-Line Career Services

(http://www.intellimatch.com) When you log on to this resume database, you become a "Watson" to your potential employer's "Holmes." Whether you like the cutesy terminology or not, the database is free for resume posters, and some high-profile companies use the site. (Since the companies post profiles, you can research them right at the site.)

Resume Zone

(http://www.careermag.com) A service of CAREERMagazine. Post your resume without charge.

Resumes on the Web

(http://www.resweb.com) This site offers several services (a resume database, your resume converted to Web format (HTML), and even promotion on the Internet) at various fee levels. There's also a job database you can search without charge.

Shawn's Internet Resume Center

(http://www.inpursuit.com/sirc) This site is primarily for those seeking jobs in corporate management, and there is a charge for posting your resume.

The Sunday Paper On-Line Resume Bulletin Board

(http://www.sundaypaper.com/wwwboard) The Sunday Paper is one big electronic classified ad section. The resume database is free.

Do You Need Your Own Web Site?

Recently, a college graduate looking for an entry-level job as an advertising illustrator was having trouble finding a position. He followed up on dozens of job leads, but in each case either his lack of experience or his highly individual illustration style cost him the job. He realized that he needed to get his work seen by as many agencies as possible—more than he could visit in person—in order to find one that was a fit. Frustrated, the young man decided to create a Web site to showcase his artwork. He registered the site with the major search engines, so that cybersurfers looking for artists and illustrators would find his site.

Within weeks, a West Coast company that specializes in the design of Web sites saw this artist's work on the Web and hired him.

Not everyone needs a personal Web site, and not every Web site will lead to a job offer. But obviously, this was one job seeker whose Web page worked for him. If you decide to take the plunge and create a site, be sure the site is really useful and professional. An error-riddled Web page can cripple a job seeker's chances just as quickly as a resume full of typos. Here are some situations where a professional and purposeful Web site may be a valuable tool in your job search:

• Your job, like the ad artist's, results in the creation of a visual product
  that can be showcased on the Web. For artists, it is especially important
  that their sites be highly visual and well designed.

• You are in a tech-savvy industry whose employers are likely to find your
  Web site. If your work involves design or the Web, then your Web site
  should be top notch and high tech.

• You are interested in pursuing job leads with employers in distant locations (since your Web site will reach employers all over the world).

If you do decide to develop a Web site, let potential employers know that it's avail-

able. Don't expect them to stumble across your Web site any more than they would just happen to run across your resume. Put your Web site address prominently on your resume. Consider sending e-mails to potential employers, inviting them to visit your Web site. Or, if you have a few dollars to invest, have a postcard made up with a sample of your work on the front and an announcement of your Web site on the back.

DON'T
Count on the
Classifieds,
BUT...

CHAPTER SIX

*Classified ads are the obvious place to look. Too old and too obvious, some people say. These skeptics say you might as well **skip** the classified ads, because they're filled with lousy jobs and bogus come-ons that only a **clueless** job seeker would be interested in.*

We say listen to the ancient sages who advised moderation in all things. Certainly, the classified ads are no longer the one-best-place to look for job openings. But they are worth investigating, as are the other published-on-paper sources of job leads you'll learn about in this chapter.

What You Should Know about the Classifieds

- Only about 15 percent of all job openings ever appear in the classified ads.

- Most of the jobs that do appear in the classified sections are not to-die-for jobs. Many are entry-level, part-time, or commission-only jobs.

- Some "jobs" that appear in the classifieds aren't jobs at all, but attempts to lure unemployed (and possibly desperate) people into various schemes and scams. (See the sidebar "Don't Get Blindsided by Blind Ads.")

- A classified ad may bring well over 1,000 responses, which means your odds of landing an interview are slim.

That said, the classifieds are a solid source of information. And you can increase your odds of surviving the resume screening if you know how to read the ads and how to respond to them, as well as the best places to look for classifieds.

Where to Find Them

The two main sources of classified ads are newspapers and trade publications.

Newspapers' Sunday editions have by far the biggest classified sections of the week; some ads run only on Sundays. But check the classifieds every day, at least for a week or two, to get the big picture.

Your local daily newspaper is a good starting place, but it is not the only place to find classified ads. The *National Business Employment Weekly*, published by the company that publishes *The Wall Street Journal*, carries ads for hundreds of business jobs in each issue. It also has articles and information about jobs and careers. You can find it at some newsstands. Short-term subscriptions are available. (Call 1-800-JOB-HUNT, or find subscription information on the Web at http://www.nbew.com.)

The *Chicago Tribune*, *The Los Angeles Times*, *The New York Times*, and the *Washington Post* are essentially national newspapers and carry classifieds for jobs nationwide. They are available at newsstands all over the country, and collectively on the Web at www.CareerPath.com. You can also visit them individually at the following addresses:

- *Chicago Tribune:* http://www.chicago.tribune.com

- *The Los Angeles Times:* http://www.latimes.com

- *The New York Times:* http://www.nytimes.com

- *The Washington Post:* http://www.washington-post.com

The *San Jose (California) Mercury News* is a treasure trove of help-wanted classified ads for people in a high-technology industry. Because employers all over the country know there's a huge pool of qualified high-tech applicants in the San Jose area, they advertise tech jobs in this newspaper. Web address: http://www.sjmercury.com.

While big-city daily newspapers are generally the best sources of classifieds, there are situations where it is worthwhile to check small-town papers. If you'd like to work for a small company, you'll find that they sometimes advertise jobs only in the communities where they are located. These small-town papers will take some effort to find. You may need to visit a library in the town where the paper is published or pay for a by-mail subscription.

Trade publications are the other major source of classified help-wanted ads. If you don't know the names of the major trade publications in your industry, a trade organization or professional association can steer you to them. In fact, these magazines and journals are often published by trade organizations. You'll find a list in most almanacs. Or you can scan the list at http://www.yahoo.com/Business_and_Economy/Organizations.

Once you identify the major trade publications in your industry, look for them at newsstands and public or university libraries. If you don't find them there, you'll need to subscribe. Many offer short-term subscriptions, and it's a good idea to read your industry's trade publications anyway. You'll find detailed, useful information that doesn't appear in the general media.

DISPLAY ADS

Display ads are large ads—they may be up to a full page but are more often one-quarter page or less—placed by big companies with many jobs to fill.

They give more details about the jobs offered, qualifications sought, and so on, than regular classifieds. If you see a display ad about a job that matches your p.p.s., it is probably worth following up on.

The company is spending serious money to advertise job openings, so it is serious about hiring. Get your resume in immediately; even though there may be many openings, these ads draw lots of responses.

Don't Get Blindsided by Blind Ads

Blind ads, also called box ads, are classified ads that don't give a company name, just a box number to respond to. A blind ad may be a lead to a perfectly legitimate job opening. Or it may be:

- A scam to get your name, address, and telephone number, which will then be used to try to sell you something or involve you in a pyramid scheme. These schemes play on the fears of people who are out of work and so desperate for an income that they are disposed to believe even the most unbelievable-sounding promises of easy money.

- A "fake ad" placed by an employment agency or other firm that, in fact, does not have a job opening but wants to collect resumes so it can tell employers that it has huge numbers of qualified job candidates.

- A fake ad placed by a company as bait. In this case, the company wants to find out who, within its own ranks, is a flight risk. It dangles a blind ad for a tantalizing job (which doesn't really exist) to see if it can lure any would-be deserters out of hiding. It's diabolical, but it happens. (Even a legitimate blind ad placed by your current employer, with the sole purpose of filling a real job opening, can cause you trouble. If you don't want your employer to know you're looking elsewhere, answering a blind ad is a risk.)

- A job opening, all right, but with a company that nobody in town wants to work for. For example, the company may be known for low pay or bad business practices and wants to camouflage its identity as much as possible for as long as possible.

Final note: Very occasionally, a prestigious employer uses a blind ad to advertise a truly terrific job. Since many people are leery of blind ads, the employer thus avoids the stampede that would occur if the whole world knew what a great company was behind the ad. The ad may be for a wonderful opening that, for whatever reason, the company doesn't want to broadcast. So, you never know.

Besides being focused on one industry, the classified ads in trade publications usually offer a higher proportion of jobs for established workers, as opposed to entry-level positions.

How to Read the Classifieds

- For at least the first week, scan all the help-wanted ads, reading all the headlines and every ad that is for a job in your industry. You'll probably find that positions matching the job you are seeking are listed under more than one category and with different job titles. This is because different companies use different names for the same job. By reading the classifieds, you'll learn about these differing job classifications and be more knowledgeable about the lingo used in your industry.

  You will also learn what companies in your industry are hiring. This is valuable knowledge, because companies that have job openings may have openings for the kind of job you want, even if those particular openings are not being advertised.

  Other information to watch for: What skills and qualifications show up in ad after ad? (The answer tells you what is in demand, and therefore what to emphasize in your cover letters, resume, and interviews.) What are the low, medium, and high salary levels for the job you are seeking? (This is information you will need when you receive an offer and begin negotiating your compensation package.)

- Watch for ads that disappear and then reappear a week or more later. This probably means either that the employer did not fill the position during the initial ad run or that the person hired did not work out. Either way, this is an employer who may well be willing to compromise on qualifications, salary, and/or other issues. If you don't meet the exact qualifications stated in the ad but can do the job (and can convince the employer that you can), go for it.

- Also, watch for slight changes in the wording of an ad. They can give you insight into what the employer has been seeing from applicants, what has been missing from the resumes received, and so on.

JOB HOTLINES: COMPANY CLASSIFIEDS BY PHONE

Some employers—especially large companies—provide job hotlines you can call to get information about current openings. Check the company's listing in the white pages of the telephone book to see if a job hotline number is listed. If not, call the main number and ask if such a hotline exists.

• The best way to track ads is to hold on to each day's (or each issue's) classified section. That way, you can always look back to see which ads have reappeared, which ones have changed, when a given ad first appeared, and so on.

• Some experts recommend that in addition to reading current ads, you should go to a library and read a few classified ad sections that are three to six months old. The idea is to look for ads for plum jobs, and respond to them. Why? Because a certain number of the people hired for these great jobs will have washed out for one reason or another. The company may not be running ads for the jobs again, since using ads didn't bring in a successful employee the first time. If you decide to follow up on such ads, you may or may not want to give away how you found out about the jobs. One alternative is to work your network until you find someone who knows about the company and can be a second source of information about the job opening. That way, you can honestly say that you heard about the opening through your network. You may get some helpful inside information at the same time.

How to Respond to a Classified Ad

• First and foremost, remember your p.p.s. As you read through hundreds of classifieds, you will no doubt see job openings that aren't what you are really looking for but are jobs that you could do. You will be tempted to think, "Look at all these jobs! Surely I can get one of them! I can do this stuff! I'll just respond to 50 of these ads, and something is sure to come through!"

Finding Out-of-Town Newspapers

If you're looking for a job in a different city or state than where you live, you'll need to read the classified ad sections of out-of-town papers. Here are some ways to find them:

- Most newspapers now have an electronic edition on the Web. At AJR Newslink (http://www.newslink.org/ daily/html), sponsored by the *American Journalism Review,* you'll find newspapers published in all 50 states and in several cities in most states. Or search the Web using the name of the newspaper you're looking for as your keyword.

- Newsstands carry some out-of-town papers, but usually only those published in major cities.

- Almost all newspapers offer by-mail subscriptions (every day or Sunday only). If you're moving to a new area and want to learn about it, a subscription is probably a good investment. The drawback is that it takes a few days for the paper to reach you; your responses to ads won't be immediate.

- Libraries subscribe to newspapers—the bigger the library, the more newspapers you'll find. But libraries, too, get their out-of-town papers by mail.

In the first place, something isn't sure to come through. Remember the odds you face when you answer an ad. If the job isn't what you're really looking for, chances are you're not as qualified as scores of other people who will respond.

In the second place, remember: This is your life. You have a plan and a target that you chose carefully to fit your life and your goals. Keep aiming at the target!

- Before you send your resume, do some research on the company. If at all possible, check out the company's Web site. If the site includes a listing of job openings, compare what you see there to what appears in the company's classifieds. You may find more information on the Web site than in the classified ad, since the employer pays for the ad on a per-word basis. You also may find information that will help you craft an attention-getting cover letter or customize your resume. One example: If the ad doesn't give the name of the person you should send your resume to (often ads give only a job title or a department name), you may be able to find that information at the Web site. And if your resume is the one out of 100 that shows up addressed to the right individual, that should give you an edge. The employer will know you were smart enough, and committed enough, to track down the information.

- See the publications listed in chapter one for more places to find information about companies, including the names of managers and executives.

- Make sure your resume uses keywords that appear in the ad. This will probably mean that you'll have to customize your resume, producing a handful of different versions that use different keywords.

- Do send a personal cover letter along with your resume, unless the ad specifically says to send only a resume. Keep the letter very brief. The cardinal rule of writing a cover letter in response to a classified ad is: Don't give them any reason to screen you out. Anything you say that doesn't relate directly to the wording of the ad may be used against you; don't say it. Refer to the keywords and requirements listed in the ad, and explain briefly that you meet or exceed them. (You do, or you wouldn't be writing this letter.)

Do mention the publication in which you saw the ad and its date. This helps the employer, who wants to know which ads are "pulling." It also gives you a record of this information (because you will keep a copy of the cover letter).

- Some ads request that you state salary requirements. Conventional wisdom says you never mention salary before the interview, and even then you try to get the employer to name a figure first. But if the ad requests that you state a salary and you don't, you could be screened out. What to do? There are several options, and you should pick the one that makes the most sense on a case by case basis. You may not want to mention salary even if you're asked to, or you can acknowledge the request but refuse to state a figure, instead saying something like, "salary required would depend on the scope of responsibilities and on the overall compensation package"; or, more simply, "salary negotiable." Finally, you can hedge your bets by stating a salary range along with the "depending on" clause.

  If the ad asks you to give your salary history, you may as well go ahead and give it. The employer almost certainly has a pretty good idea of the salary range for your current or most recent job anyway.

- If the ad gives a fax number, it's there because the company prefers to receive resumes by fax. If it's not there, respond to the mailing address given. Since overnight delivery is very expensive, it's probably best to go with regular mail. A high-prestige or luxury-oriented company where extravagance is the norm might be an exception.

- Follow up by phone a week after sending your resume, but don't make a pest of yourself. If you are told no decision has been made yet, ask approximately when they expect to decide. Let whomever you are talking with know you are still very interested in the opening, and then get off the line. If an ad states "no phone calls please," you should always honor this request.

- Some ads ask you to respond by phone. If so, remember that the person on the other end of the line has one mission: to screen out applicants. Again, anything you say can be used against you, so you must say as little as possible. If the employer begins asking you questions about yourself and your qualifications, say you are on a short break at work (or give a similar, truthful reason) and can't talk at length but would be happy to come and talk with the employer in person. If she declines, ask about sending your resume. If the person still tries to question you, say, "I'm very sorry, but my break time is up. Thank you for your time." Then, if you have enough information, go ahead and fax or mail your resume. Don't make any reference to having called. (On the other hand, if you were invited to send your resume, mention this in your cover letter.)

- In general, you should respond to an ad immediately. If you're responding by fax, send your fax the day you read the ad, or the next morning. If you're using the mail, send your resume and cover letter as soon as you can get them ready—the next day if possible. Because of the large number of resumes companies receive in response to ads, they may never even look at those that arrive after a certain point. The cutoff point may be a certain number of days after an ad has run, or it may be when the mountain of resumes received reaches a certain height. In any case, the sooner yours arrives, the better.

- Be sure to keep a record of your responses to ads. Keep a copy of each cover letter, as every one will be different. If you have several versions of your resume, make a note on your copy of the cover letter to remind you which version went out with that letter.

Other Print Sources of Job Leads

The business section of the newspaper is a valuable source of information and job leads. Read it regularly. Many newspapers publish special, expanded business sections on Mondays. Look for news of companies that are growing, new companies moving into your area, and other signals of potential job openings. Also read the columns that report the hirings, promotions, and job changes of managers and executives. Keep

track of who works where in your industry, whose career seems headed for the stratosphere, and so on. Managers who are promoted or who change jobs sometimes hire people—especially assistants and other support staff—as soon as they make the change. It makes sense to send your resume to managers in your industry who are on the move.

Finally, don't forget to let your fingers do the walking through your local Yellow Pages. They provide an at-a-glance inventory of which companies in your industry do business in your area. Yellow Pages ads also can be scanned for other information, such as how long the company has been in business and exactly what products and services it sells.

The bottom line: Print sources still provide a wealth of information that clued-in job seekers can't afford to overlook. After all, look how much you've learned from reading this book!

GETTING the most out of RECRUITERS

This may surprise you; it is a common misunderstanding that often allows people working with recruiters to be far too passive in their job search, waiting for recruiters to call, and far too dependent on recruiters to help them change jobs or change careers. Recruiters are in the business of providing their clients with specific hiring objectives. If your background and experience match the particular assignment a recruiter is working on, a recruiter can be very helpful. But don't expect him to do the tough work involved in finding the job that is right for you. This chapter will tell you just what recruiters—who are sometimes called headhunters—do, how they can help you, how they can hurt you, and how to handle these often-misunderstood creatures.

Can a Recruiter Help You?

A recruiter is most likely to be a boon to your career if you're already something of a standout. Recruiters and the companies that hire them operate under two fundamental assumptions: One, the best person for a job probably already has a job, and a good one. Two, a person who comes to us is probably not the person we want. When it comes to working with a recruiter, you are faced with a paradox: The harder you try, the less likely you are to succeed!

The vast majority of jobs handled by recruiters pay well. If you haven't been making at least $60,000 a year, you'll probably have a hard time getting the attention of a recruiter. The more you earn, the more likely it is that a good recruiter will be willing to invest some time in you and your career. (If you're wondering why, it has to do with how recruiters get paid. Details to come.)

In addition, recruiters are interested in known quantities, someone with a track record of specific, concrete accomplishments. This is because they are working for clients with specific objectives. Recruiters and employers figure that if you can do it for Company A, you can do it for Company B. On the other hand, they figure that if you haven't done it yet, maybe you can't do it. And recruiters must deliver a person who can do the job. Their reputations depend on it.

Traditionally, recruiters (like employers) preferred people with a long history in one industry, a history that allowed them to develop a core set of skills to a high level. As the overall job market has become more fluid—employers now recognize that many important skills transfer from one industry to another, and career-changing has become more accepted—recruiters, too, have become more welcoming to career-changers. But they still like to see people who demonstrate stability, continuity, highly developed skills, and impressive achievements. As a general rule of thumb, don't count on a recruiter to help you change careers; recruiters most often work with people moving within the same industry or job function.

Recruiters are more interested in people who are employed than in people who are not. The thinking is that really strong candidates are sure to be recognized and prized by their current employers; they're not likely to be among the victims of downsizings, layoffs, outplacements, and other ugly compound words. In a recruiter's mind, if you were dispensable, then you're...well, dispensable.

Keep Reading!

If you didn't see yourself in the preceding paragraphs, don't stop reading yet. There are exceptions to all of the above, and even recruiters know it. Some recruiting agencies do handle jobs in the $25,000 to $40,000 range. These same agencies are likely to handle at least some entry-level and early-career jobs that don't require a long list of previous achievements. And there are situations when a recruiter is interested in a candidate who is not currently employed. For example, your entire department was axed, even the best and brightest. Or, maybe your company downsized but, recognizing your great value, offered you a plum job in another state; you're on the street only because you declined to relocate, knowing your skills and accomplishments would land you another good job right where you are.

Whether you're the exception or the rule, a recruiter is going to be interested in you and able to help you if there's something special and marketable about you. If you helped your current or previous employer successfully implement a new technology that other companies also need to implement, that's special and marketable. If you've sold everything from candy bars to cars and collected a wall-full of "top salesperson" plaques along the way, that's special and marketable, too.

What Does a Recruiter Have That You Need?

If you're such a standout, why do you need a recruiter? Well, there are things a good recruiter can do for you that you can't do for yourself, even if you are a star.

For starters, good recruiters have connections to job openings that nobody else knows about. (To find out why, keep reading.)

Second, good recruiters are excellent sources of information about your industry. A good recruiter can offer sound advice on job decisions and on managing your career. The best recruiter can help you make a strategic move that will be good for you now, and a good long-term career move as well.

What a recruiter can't do is replace you as commanding officer of your job search. No matter how good your recruiter is, no matter how enthusiastic she is about you, no matter how sure she is that you're perfect for the assignment she's handling, don't rely

solely on her to get you leads and interviews. You must keep working hard on the other fronts of your job search.

The Recruitment Process (and Who Pays for It)

Employers pay recruiters to find the people they need to hire. Since recruiters handle the research, advertising, screening, preliminary interviewing, skills testing, and background checking, employers save time and avoid costly hiring mistakes. Employers also minimize the risk of all-out war with other employers by hiring mercenaries to do their headhunting for them, rather than doing it themselves.

Recruiting firms almost always have one of two arrangements with the employers they serve. Either the recruiting firm is on a retainer, or the firm receives a fee (called a contingency fee and essentially the same as a commission) each time it introduces the employer to an applicant who is hired. Under both arrangements, the recruiter's fee is a percentage of the new hire's annual salary—about 1/3 of the annual salary is the industry average for a retainer firm; contingency firms typically earn less. The recruiter doesn't get paid unless the new hire stays on the job for a minimum period of time, usually 60 to 90 days. In a retained search, the search firm has to replace the individual if he leaves within a certain period of time, typically a year. This fee arrangement emphasizes the importance of finding the right person for the job.

In general, firms that work on retainer recruit executives and other highly paid professionals who earn at least $75,000 a year. They are retained by employers because of their expertise in selecting highly qualified candidates for specific jobs. In contrast, contingency recruiters are paid only if they fill the position and do not typically have exclusive arrangements with the employer.

The two kinds of firms have different kinds of relationships with job-seekers, as well. A retainer firm's goal is to find the best person for its client's needs. This means that a recruiter at a retainer firm will represent you to only one client at a time. He won't promote you to other clients that have similar jobs available; this would be seen as a conflict by the clients who pay him.

Conversely, a contingency agency's goal is to place you somewhere, so that it collects its fee. Its recruiter may shop your resume to any and every company that has the kind of job you're looking for. At first this might sound helpful. But there can be very real drawbacks to working with contingency agencies. You'll find what you need to know about managing your relationship with either kind of recruiter in "Watching Out for Your Own Best Interests," below.

You'll notice that we haven't said anything about agencies where you, the job-seeker, pay the recruiter. That's because legitimate recruiting agencies are paid by employers, not by job-hunters. (See the sidebars "This Is a Scam" and "This Is Not a Scam.")

Finding the Right Recruiting Firm for You

There are about 3,000 recruiting firms in the United States. Some are generalists, working with all kinds of employers and job-seekers. Others specialize by industry, by job level, and/or by region. You'll need to do some research to find the right agency for you.

Many contingency recruiting firms specialize in one industry, such as health care, high-tech, or management. This is because it is efficient for them to get to know one industry in depth—its companies, its people, and its needs—and to concentrate their efforts there. If a contingency recruiter tries to place you at one company and it doesn't work out, the chances are good that the recruiter knows of other companies with similar needs.

Retainer firms are less likely to be industry-specialized, but more likely to specialize in recruiting for high-paying, managerial and executive jobs.

If you are not limiting your job search to one city, or if you are hoping to make a long-distance move, your best bet is a recruiting agency that is affiliated or networked with other agencies nationwide. Such affiliations are likely to be prominently featured in the agency's advertisements and brochures. If they're not, be skeptical of a recruiter's assurances that she can represent you to companies outside your area.

To find the agency that is most likely to have the job leads that match your p.p.s., start

This Is a Scam

 There, amid the hundreds of tiny ads for part-time, third-shift stock clerks and commission-only sales jobs, you spy a beacon of hope. The big headline type reads:

"Dozens of Unadvertised Jobs!"

"Salaries Up to $200,000!"

The ad is placed by a "career consulting" firm that promises inside-track access to the kinds of high-status, high-paying jobs that mere mortals like yourself somehow never manage to find on your own.

Sounds like a great shortcut to your brilliant new career, you think. There's probably a catch—you're not that clueless, after all—but it can't hurt to give them a call.

You call. The voice on the other end of the phone is enthusiastic and friendly. It asks a few questions about your background. Yes, it says, you sound like the kind of person we're looking for.

When you go for your first visit, the office oozes luxury from the plush carpet to the high ceiling. Velvet sofas, leather armchairs, "consultants" who look like they just stepped out of Vogue and GQ.

And they like you! They only work with a very exclusive group of candidates, they assure you, and you qualify! For the reasonable fee of $5,000 (sometimes less, sometimes more), they will prepare you to apply for and land the exalted jobs they know are available. And you don't even have to pay the whole $5,000 up front; they'll take $2,000 down. They don't mind waiting for the rest of their money, they tell you, because virtually 100 percent of their clients land high-paying jobs.

> While your eyes are still swimming with stars, you are asked to sign a contract. You sign, and hand over a check, relieved that all that endless writing of cover letters is behind you.
>
> Your career counselor ushers you into yet another velvety office where you're given some resume templates, interviewing tips, and lists of industry contacts. (All of which you could have gotten in this book, by the way.) And…that's it! You're on your own! Good luck, sucker!
>
> When you actually read the contract, you'll find that it doesn't guarantee anything, except that you'll pay the company the rest of the money you owe.
>
> And the moral of the story is: Thou shalt not pay anyone to get you a job.

by checking your network. Ask people if they have ever worked with a recruiter or know of agencies that specialize in your industry. Also check published sources of information about recruiters.

Making the Connection

Connecting with the right firm is important. But how you make the connection is just as important. It's best if the recruiter comes to you. But if he doesn't, you'll need to go to him.

When You Are Approached

Be complimented. The recruiter has some reason to believe that you're marketable, or she wouldn't be spending her time calling you. But unless you already know her, proceed with caution.

The first time a recruiter calls, don't give her too much information. Be aware that the recruiter may dig for information about your current employer, as well as about you,

This Is Not a Scam: Finding a Career Counselor

If you need individualized, professional help getting on with your career, you can get it without getting scammed. The best way to begin is to call the National Board for Certified Counselors (800) 398-5389 and ask for a list of certified career counselors in your area. Certified career counselors must have a Master's Degree and three years of supervised experience in career counseling. And they never charge big up-front fees. Their hourly fees range from about $50 to $75. It is important to note there is a difference between career counselors and recruiters. Although recruiters do offer solid career advice, they are not in the career counseling business.

Career counselors do not recruit or place people in jobs. They simply provide job-seekers with the expertise they need. A good career counselor can pinpoint any problems in your resume and help you remedy them, coach you so that you perform well in interviews, and so on.

Do your homework, even when hiring a certified counselor. Ask for the names and telephone numbers of satisfied clients, and call them. Check your network, to see if anyone knows anything about the counselor. Call your local Better Business Bureau or even your state attorney general's office and ask if there have been any complaints about the person.

Once you're satisfied that the counselor is qualified, go to see him prepared with specific questions to make the best use of your time with him. Don't pay those hourly fees for information you could have found yourself at the library or on the Internet.

Where to Find Information about Recruiters

Here are some of the best sources of information about recruiters and their specialties:

The Directory of Executive Recruiters (Kennedy Publications) lists about 2,000 North American agencies and their specialties. It is available in some bookstores and libraries, or by calling the publisher at (800) 531-0007.

Executive Job-Changing Workbook (Owlet,1994), available at bookstores, has a list of recruiters.

The National Directory of Personnel Consultants by Specialization (National Association of Personnel Services) is available on paper or on disk. Call (703)684-0180.

The Recruiting & Search Report is the name of a company, not a publication. The company sells directories of recruiting firms that are organized by industry and updated quarterly. Call (904) 235-3733.

Other sources:

Check the classified section of your Sunday newspaper to see which agencies are placing ads, how large the ads are, how consistently they appear, and what kinds of jobs are offered. Remember, some agencies place ads simply to collect resumes; glowing ad copy may not be backed up by actual jobs. But these ads will give you an idea of what kinds of jobs the companies recruit for.

Check the Yellow Pages, under Employment Agencies, for the same kind of information.

HEADS UP

and be prepared to deflect all questions. You've got to check out her firm and her reputation before you become associated with her in any official way. When the recruiter calls, qualify her. Find out her expertise in your field and her experience in recruiting people like you. Ask what companies or type of companies she works with. If she is working with the best companies in your industry, chances are that she is one of the best recruiters in the industry. Once the call has ended, start digging. Begin with your network and the published sources listed above. Find the company's Web site, and also do a search to see if you can find other references to the agency on the Internet.

When you've filled in as many blanks as you can on your own, call the recruiter back and ask her for the answers you still need. Let your research show in your conversation, so the recruiter knows you're clued in.

After a qualifying conversation with the recruiter in which she will ask you questions about your background and determine if you are a candidate for the position she is trying to fill, the recruiter may dive right in to question you about your background and achievements. Or, she may quickly suggest an in-person meeting. As a general rule, do not share your resume with a recruiter until you meet her. If you can't meet with the recruiter and she insists on a resume, say something like, "Of course, since you and I haven't yet agreed to work together, my resume is for your information only. Please don't share or copy it, and of course don't present it to any employers before we get together." This should go without saying, but until you get to know this person, it's best to play it safe. Make all your communication clear and specific.

How to Evaluate a Recruitment Agency

When you are approached by a recruiter (or when you approach one) your first response should be to thoroughly research the recruiter and his agency. Here are a few questions you need answers to:

Questions about the agency:

1. Is the firm a retainer firm or a contingency firm?

2. How long has the agency been in business?

3. What are the recruiters' qualifications and backgrounds?

4. How many recruiters are on staff?

5. What clients does the recruiting firm work for and what are some representative assignments that they have recently completed?

6. Does the agency charge fees for services, from helping you write your resume to making copies of it? If so, this is not necessarily a problem. But fees should be comparable to what you would pay elsewhere for the same services, they should be services you truly need, and you should have the option to have the services done elsewhere if you prefer.

Questions about the individual recruiter:

1. What are his educational and professional qualifications? How long has he been a recruiter, how long in your industry, how long with the current firm, and how long in your area?

> 2. Perhaps the most important question to ask yourself: Do you feel
> comfortable with the recruiter and trust him to represent you to
> employers?
>
> **Red flag:**
> Beware of any agency that asks you to pay a fee. (See the sidebars
> "This Is a Scam" and "This Is Not a Scam.")

Whether it's over the phone or an in-person meeting, the recruiter should tell you about the client and the position that is open. The recruiter might not disclose the name of the client for a couple of reasons. The employer may have reasons for wanting the job's availability to be kept as confidential as possible. (Just two of many possible scenarios: It's possible that the person who is leaving the job doesn't know it yet, or that the company has ruled out in-house candidates but doesn't want them to know it is looking outside.)

Treat every discussion with a recruiter like a job interview because it is. Understand that the recruiter is there to assess you. If she represents you to her clients, you become a reflection of her work in the employer's eyes. It's important to her that, in appearance and presentation as well as in accomplishments, you make a very strong impression. Be prepared for the recruiter to grill you about your accomplishments, your reasons for leaving previous jobs, your strengths and weakness, your career goals, and so on. There are two reasons for these probing questions. One, she needs to find out whether your experience qualifies you for the position and assess whether you're a match for the job in question. Two, she needs to find out how to "sell" you to the employer and identify any possible problem areas. She'll expect you to be ready with detailed, factual answers. If you're not, she'll doubt your mental sharpness or your honesty.

Don't forget to share your p.p.s. with the recruiter. It's a great capsule explanation of who you are and what you can do.

As long as you continue to be interested in what the recruiter has to say, most of the conversation should be about the employer's needs and how you can meet them. At some point, though, it will be your turn to ask the questions. Whether you get the company's name or not, ask other, more general questions about it, such as its overall health, its plans and goals for the near future, its corporate culture, and so on. You should try to find out why the position is open if possible, and find out why the person doing the job is no longer there; this may reveal some valuable information. Pay close attention to how the recruiter answers these questions. (Take notes if possible, so that you can refer back to specifics.) Then, if and when you do get the company's name, do your own research to find out more about the company.

> ### HEADS UP
>
> When you meet a recruiter for the first time, dress as you would for a job interview. That's what the recruiter wants to see: how you will present yourself to the employer.

Some other questions you can reasonably expect a recruiter to answer: Does the recruiter have an exclusive agreement with the employer? (The answer should be yes.) How long has the search been going on? How many people at the hiring company must agree on the successful candidate?

Even if the recruiter seems very positive about you, be aware that she is required to woo you. Keep a level head, and remember that she's having this same glowing conversation with other candidates.

Getting on a Recruiter's Radar Screen

It's not good news but it's true: The mere fact that you approach a recruiter will make you less appealing to him. Recruiters are interested in the sought-after, not the seekers; in the haves, not the have-nots.

Recruiting firms receive as many as 1,000 resumes a week from people its recruiters have never heard of. A large majority of the people who send those resumes out on wings of hope never receive a reply of any kind, and it's easy to understand why. No

successful firm has the time to wade through a weekly tidal wave of unsolicited mail and send out 999 "we regret to inform you" letters. They're in the business of filling jobs, not answering mail.

So, what are you supposed to do if a recruiter hasn't called you?

- Make yourself easier to find by increasing your professional profile. This can be done in many ways—speaking at industry conferences, writing articles for trade journals, or winning important industry awards.

- Use your network to find someone who can make a connection for you. Work that network until you get to someone who will make a call to a recruiter she knows and persuade him to do one of two things: At best, call you; at least, give your resume a serious look.

  If you can't find such a person, you can always send in your resume "cold." But remember the odds. You'd be better off going back to your network and throwing your net a little wider until you catch the fish you want.

- Send in a dynamite cover letter and resume, addressed to an individual recruiter. Assuming that you have been referred by someone, put that person's name in the very first sentence of your letter. You need to separate yourself from the unknown masses immediately.

- Again, use your p.p.s. Recruiters like job-seekers who know exactly who they are and what they can do. This makes it easy for the recruiter to understand you and find a match for you.

- Fill your letter with hard facts and figures about your achievements. This tells the recruiter you're someone he can sell.

Some job-seekers mass-mail their resumes to every recruiting agency in their industry, hoping to better their odds. Most experts say this is a waste of time, money, and paper. Instead, they recommend that you send your resume to no more than the two or three agencies that are the best fit for you and your p.p.s. Send each with a personal referral, if at all possible. It's not a good idea to work with more than one contingency recruiter at a time, even if you do have that rare opportunity. This is especially true if you work in a small industry, or if there are only a few potential employers in your area. If your resume is submitted to one employer by more than one agency, the company may very well pass on hiring you in order to avoid a fight over which agency should receive the fee.

It's possible that you will do everything right—pinpoint the right recruiting agency, get a personal referral, send in a dynamite cover letter and resume, send it at the right time, and all the rest—and still not receive a response from the agency. And the reason may have nothing to do with you. One possible reason: Your current employer may be one of the firm's clients. If so, the recruiting firm won't touch you. An employer that is paying a recruiter to bring in talent would be rightfully outraged if that same recruiter were at the same time escorting talent out the door. In fact, not hearing from the firm isn't the worst thing that can happen to you in this scenario. Someone at the recruiting firm could tell your employer that you're job-hunting. It can be difficult to find out which agencies your employer works with, but it never hurts to try. In short, don't tell a recruiter anything that you wouldn't reveal in a job interview.

Watching Out for Your Own Best Interests

The key to having a successful relationship with a recruiter is to stay in the driver's seat. It's your job search; your recruiter is just one resource among many that you will use. You have the right, and the responsibility, to use that resource to your best advantage. That means you manage your recruiter, not the other way around. It means you're aware of potential problems, and how to avoid them.

Here are some areas in which problems often arise working with contingency agencies, and what you can do to prevent them.

Signing the Application Contract

Most agencies have their own, very comprehensive application forms that all candidates fill out. Many times, the application contains language that makes it a binding,

What You Should Tell Your Recruiter

- Tell your recruiter the truth. If he is successful at all, he is very good at verifying information and very well connected. If you lie, he will find out, and it will blow your chance of getting the job.

- Tell your recruiter about any problems or issues that could impact your job search or working life. Example: If, when the recruiter tells you the name of the employer he's recruiting for, you realize that the only person who ever fired you now works for that company, your recruiter needs to know. This doesn't necessarily mean you're out of the running. Give the recruiter the details about the situation. He can then do some detective work to find out if the past will affect your current prospects. He may find out that the problematic manager not only works at an out-of-town facility but is out of favor with top management.

legal contract. Read the entire contract very carefully. If it contains any statement that you don't understand or are not comfortable with, do not sign it. Feel free to ask that certain portions of the contract be changed, or to have an attorney read it and advise you.

Some specific things to watch for in applications/contracts:

- Don't sign an application that gives a recruiter the exclusive right to place you. Under such an agreement, if you find a job on your own, with no help or involvement on the part of the recruiter, you could be legally required to pay the recruiter a fee.

What You Shouldn't Tell Your Recruiter

- Don't tell your recruiter anything negative or unprofessional about an employer he sends you to see. The recruiter works for the employer.

- Don't tell your recruiter about any personal problems or issues that have no relevance to your job search or working life. Such things are none of his business. If he passes them on, they could hurt you professionally for years to come.

- Don't sign an application that states that when you accept a job offer you are required to stay in the position for a certain period of time. According to their own contracts with employers, agencies don't receive their fees unless hirees stay on the job for a minimum period of time. To protect themselves from losing their fee if you quit or are fired, some recruiting agencies put this "must stay" requirement in their contracts with job-seekers. This passes the risk on to you, making you liable for the fee if you leave the job for any reason (including reasons beyond your control, such as being laid off).

- Don't sign an application that locks you into a long, exclusive relationship with a recruiter. You want to be free to move on after a few weeks if the recruiter isn't working well with you, or doesn't seem trustworthy. Don't get stuck with a months-long commitment. And remember, the exclusivity agreement should clearly refer only to other recruiters, not to your own job-seeking efforts. Don't sign an application that makes you liable for paying the recruiter a fee for a job you land on your own.

Working with Contingency Agencies

Contingency agencies often market job-seekers to several companies at once. This approach offers the possibility of fast placement, but it can also create problems. Most problems arise in situations where the recruiter does not have a written agreement with the employer, giving him the exclusive right to recruit applicants for the position. Here are a couple of examples of how this can hurt you:

- **Problem:** Let's say that your recruiter arranges for you to interview for a job that matches your p.p.s. beautifully. You do well in the interview and are called back for a second, where you also impress. At this point, you're probably feeling rather confident that the job is yours. But a week goes by and you don't hear anything. Then, the following Monday, a letter arrives from the employer telling you that, although you were a top candidate, someone else has been hired.

  What happened? Well, it's possible that the only difference between you and the person who was hired was that the other person wasn't working with a contingency recruiter and, therefore, was cheaper. (Remember, the employer would have had to pay the recruiter up to one-third of your annual salary.)

  Prevention: Have your recruiter sign an agreement with you, guaranteeing that she will present you only to employers with whom she has an exclusive agreement.

- **Problem:** Let's say you are working with a contingency recruiter, and are also finding and following up on jobs leads yourself. (And that's exactly what you should be doing.) One of your leads turns into an interview and, eventually, into a job offer. But when you accept the job, the recruiter claims she is owed a fee because she presented your resume to the same employer without your knowledge. If you can't prove that you contacted the employer first and independently of the recruiter, you could be held liable for her fee.

  Prevention: You may want to have your recruiter sign an agreement with you, guaranteeing that she will send your resume or otherwise "pitch" you only to one, specified employer for one, specified job opening. This slows down the placement process. (In effect, you are using the contingency agency like a retainer agency.) But it protects your own job-hunting activities against poaching by the recruiter. If you want your recruiter to promote you to several employers, be sure to use the alternate prevention strategy below.

Double Prevention: Keep detailed records of all of your contacts with both employers and your recruiter. Keep copies of all correspondence and other documents, and take notes (and date them) about every telephone call and personal meeting. If a contingency agency claims it is due a fee when you are hired, you can prove that you contacted the company before the recruiter did.

Setting Up Interviews

A recruiter's goal should be to place you in the job that's right for you. Sending you on a lot of interviews won't get either of you to the goal if they're not the right interviews.

When a recruiter sends you to interview for jobs for which you're overqualified, underqualified, or just not right (remember your p.p.s.), she's wasting your time and the employers' time. She's not opening the right doors for you.

If you encounter this problem, have a talk with your recruiter. Remind her of your p.p.s. and your commitment to it. If the problem continues, move on to another recruiter.

Negotiating Your Compensation

The recruiter needs to understand your compensation history and expectations in order to accurately represent you to her client. The most important rules are: Be honest and be realistic with your compensation expectations. Your recruiter may come with you to your interview with the employer, and may even play a mediating role in negotiating your compensation. Remember that the recruiter's greater loyalty is to the employer who pays her.

You can prevent this situation by not telling the recruiter exactly what compensation package you want, which parts of the package are important to you and which aren't, and so on. If she doesn't know what you want, she can't control the negotiations.

What If You Don't Want the Job?

When you receive a job offer, it will come after the recruiter has invested considerable time, energy, and effort in the match. He's done his job, and he's looking forward to receiving the reward that comes his way when you sign on.

But what if you decide you don't want the job?

The recruiter will not be happy. He should remain professional, but don't expect him to be happy. Not only did his paycheck just fly out the window (unless he's on retainer), but he has to tell his client that she can't have what she wants (even if he is on retainer).

To minimize bad feeling, you must:

- Say you don't want the job as soon as you know you don't want it. Don't cause the recruiter to continue to invest time in something that's not going to happen. Don't leave the recruiter and the employer pinched for time to recruit another candidate.

- Tell the recruiter that you're very sorry it wasn't the right job for you, and mean it. Be prepared to explain why it wasn't the right job.

- Steer the recruiter to another strong candidate if you possibly can.

THE *Interview* is your *chance* TO SHINE

CHAPTER EIGHT

*If you work at your job search and work at it wisely—creating your p.p.s., writing a **superb** resume, working your network, and all the rest—employers will begin to open their doors to you.*

Your resume and cover letter will make employers want to meet you in person and find out if you're really the kind of person who:

• Can do the job

• Can do more than the job

• Will fit in with the company's people, values, and goals

Answering these questions is the purpose of every job interview. No matter what questions you are asked, they all stem from the employer's desire to know these three things about you. Therefore, all you have to do in any interview is convince the

employer that the answers are yes, yes, and yes. And, of course, that your yeses are bigger and better than anybody else's yeses.

It's not easy, but you can do it. Now that you know exactly what an employer needs to know about you before she can say yes, you're already considerably more clued in than a lot of your competition. And we're just getting started. The rest of this chapter tells you everything you need to know to turn the interview into a job offer.

Preparing for the Interview

Preparation isn't everything, but it's almost everything. Before you walk into the interview, you've got to know the company as if you already work there, know how you'll answer the inevitable tough questions, and much more. It's a lot of work. The upside is that when you know you've got it all mastered, you can walk in the door confident and ready to show that you're the best person for the job.

Do Your Research

When you are invited to interview for a job, the first thing you must do is gather information—plenty of it.

First, you need to get some basic information from the person who calls to schedule the interview. This includes:

- Where will the interview be held and how do you get there?

- Who will be interviewing you (their names and titles)? One person, or more? Simultaneously, or one after another? (If this is going to be a marathon, you want to know.) Will the person who would be your immediate supervisor be there?

- What kind of interview will it be: a preliminary interview, or a decision-making interview that could result in a job offer?

Now you're on your own. Look back at the "Company Profile" sidebar in chapter one

on page 29. If you have not already created a profile for the company you'll be interviewing with, do it now. Then expand the profile by adding even more information.

Go back to your network to get up-to-date, inside information about the company and about the department you're interviewing with. Through your network, try to find and talk with both current employees and former employees who have left fairly recently. (Former employees, especially, can give you very honest, though not always objective, information. Ask them why they left the company.) Get as much information as you can about managers, problems, plans, and so on. (If you're not sure how to dress for the interview, these are good people to ask.) Be professional and positive. Through the grapevine, it may get back to the person who is going to interview you that you are asking around about the company. That's not a problem as long as your questions are reasonable and your intent is friendly.

Search at least a year's back issues of general business and trade publications for mentions of the company. You're looking for information about problems the company has faced (for example, a recall of its products or a major lawsuit), changes it has made (selling a subsidiary, moving its headquarters, changing its advertising), and its place in the industry (slipping in the face of new competition?).

Check out the company's Web site. Other sources, such as the news media, give you the outside world's view of the company. The Web site gives you the company's view of itself. Read between the lines to get solid clues about the corporate culture.

If the site invites you to request a copy of the company's annual report or other literature, do it. (If such material is not offered at the Web site, call the Human Resources department to request it. Just explain that you are preparing for your interview.)

Check out job openings listed on the site. Is the job you're interviewing for listed? Does the listing give a salary? Is there a date showing when the job was first posted? This information can be valuable. If the position has been open for a long time, you can ask why at the interview. (Try to find out from your network ahead of time, too, and see how the two answers match up.) Maybe you have a skill the employer has been unable to find in previous candidates. Emphasizing that skill in the interview may get you a job offer. If the job is offered to you, you may have more leverage to negotiate a higher salary as well.

Recheck salary surveys (see the sidebar "Salary Surveys" in chapter five) to remind yourself what the range is for the job at hand. Then do your best to find out how this company pays in general: low, average, or high. (Back to your network.) This will give you an idea of what to expect if you are offered a job and how to respond to the initial offer.

HOW RESEARCH PAID OFF FOR JONATHAN

Remember Jonathan, who landed a job as a customer care representative with a high-tech communications company? (See chapter one.) His preinterview research played a big role in getting him the job. By checking the company's Web site, Jonathan found out what stores sold the company's products. Then he went to a store and checked out all the products.

When the interviewer explained to Jonathan that the company needed people to serve its cellular phone customers, Jonathan knew all about the phones: how many models were available, what features each model had, and so on. The interviewer was understandably impressed.

Your preinterview research might even include a visit to the building where the interview will be held. This may be the only way to make sure that you know how to get there and how long the drive will take. Also, do some people-watching, to see how employees dress.

There's one more place to do research: your resume. Take a fresh look at the skills, experience, and accomplishments you listed. Think through how you can apply them to what you have learned about the company's needs. Example: Ron Smith's resume listed his skills in hand-applied fabric printing techniques. In researching Sam K. Designs before his interview there, Ron learned that the company was about to open its first overseas production facility in Indonesia. Goal: to produce fabrics using traditional methods such as batik. Ron knew the company would need someone who could create designs that would be appropriate for these production methods. And he knew that that someone was him.

All this information will serve you in many ways once you get to the interview. You'll be ready to respond to questions with specifics about how your skills and experiences can be assets to the company. You'll be able to talk about the company's challenges and plans, and how you fit into

them. You'll show that you're willing to work by the amount of work you've put in before you've even been offered a job. Thorough research will equip you to prove that you can do the job, you can do more than the job, and that you will fit in.

Decide What You Will Wear

Wearing the right "uniform" to the interview is one way to show that you fit in. The old saying "you never get a second chance to make a first impression" still holds true.

If a suit is what you need, deciding what to wear is easy; there are some pretty universal guidelines to follow. But, of course, a suit may not be what you need. If you're a creative type (a musician, an advertising artist, or a fabric designer, for example), a suit is almost certainly too traditional. You're expected to wear your creativity on your sleeve, if you will. If you're interviewing for a job as the manager of a tree nursery, a suit is a sure way to look out of place. No matter what you are wearing, your shoes should be polished and your nails neatly manicured.

Best advice: Dress as you would if you were showing up for your first day of work. To say it another way, dress a little more conservatively, a little more formally than you would normally dress for the

THE UNIFORM

If your interview calls for a traditional suit, here are some guidelines.

Men

- Suit: black, navy, or charcoal wool; navy or light gray in a lightweight, natural fabric if it is summer
- Shirt: white or light blue cotton, long-sleeved
- Tie: silk, in a dark, muted pattern that coordinates with your suit
- Socks: match pants
- Shoes: polished black leather dress shoes

Women

- Suit: black, navy or charcoal wool, knee-length skirt
- Shirt: white or light-blue cotton, long-sleeved
- Stockings: flesh-toned
- Shoes: low heels in black (or to match suit)
- Makeup: natural-looking

job. Remember, to find out how you would normally dress, do your research. If all else fails, call the Human Resources department and ask. You may feel silly, but not as silly as you'll feel if you show up dressed inappropriately. Besides, no one is going to fault you for making an effort to fit in. In fact, that's just what the employer wants you to do.

No matter what you wear, wear very little jewelry. For both men and women, a businesslike watch and a wedding band are fine. Women may add simple earrings and a simple gold or pearl necklace.

Most experts say to avoid perfume and aftershave. Some people feel they don't belong in the workplace at all. In any case, scent is highly subjective. Why risk losing out on a job because your interviewer hates your cologne or, worse yet, is allergic to it?

A note about casual Friday: For you, it's not, unless your interviewer specifically tells you to dress casually. If your current office has casual Fridays and your potential employer doesn't, then try to avoid scheduling a Friday interview.

Get Your Things Together: What to Bring

When you pack your leather briefcase (and it will almost always be a briefcase, not a purse or a backpack) for your job interview, don't forget to include:

- Directions to the interview and the exact address, including the floor number and suite number, if any

- The name and telephone number of the interviewer, in case something extreme happens and you have to call to tell him you will be late

- A few copies of your resume

- A few copies of your reference sheet

- Business cards, if you have them

- Your questions about the job

- A legal pad and a pen

- Samples of your work if this applies to your job and if you have been asked to bring them or think you might have an opportunity to show them

If you want to bring a purse, try to fit it inside your briefcase so you don't look overburdened.

What Not to Bring:

- Your cellular phone or pager. Some things are too important to be interrupted, and a job interview is one of them.

- Your children or pets. Laugh if you like, but it has happened.

Put Yourself in the Interviewer's Shoes

One important step in preparing for your interview is to put yourself in the interviewer's place for a while. Hiring people is one of the most important jobs in any organization. Hiring the wrong person can have dire consequences.

Hire someone who, it turns out, can't do the job, and you've cost the company time and money. Productivity may lag. Customers may take their business elsewhere. If you've got to fire the person you never should have hired, you've got to repeat the hiring process and repair the damage. And you've got to explain to your own boss how you could have made such a huge mistake in the first place.

RESEARCH CHECKLIST

What You Must Know Before You Go:

- How to get there and how long the commute will take

- How you should dress

- Who will be interviewing you

- What the company's (and/or department's) main problems, challenges, and goals are; how you can contribute to solving or reaching them

- Anything that has had the company in the news in the past year

- Questions you will ask about the job

- What salary and benefits are likely to be offered

Hire someone who has the skills to do the job but not the will or the character, and you can have even bigger problems. What if you hire a perfectly competent person who also happens to be an embezzler, or who only shows up for work half the time, or who gets angry and threatens coworkers? Again, you're going to have to fire him and start over—and hope he doesn't sue you or try to run you over with his car. It will take years to regain your boss's confidence after that kind of fiasco.

And you thought *you*, the interviewee, had worries!

The point of this little exercise is to understand what the interviewer needs from you, and give it to her. She needs assurance that you're going to be good for the company and therefore good for her. She needs to believe that for years to come, every time she sees you in the elevator, she will think, "Ah, Bill. Hiring him was the smartest thing I've ever done!" Everything you do and say in the interview should help create that vision in her mind.

Practice Makes Perfect

Now that you're mentally prepared for the interview, it's time for some dress rehearsals. Make your practice interviews as much like the real thing as you can. Dress exactly as you will dress for the interview. (That way, you won't discover an hour before the actual interview that the store hemmed your pants too short.) If possible, borrow someone's office to use as your set. Take everything with you that you will take to the actual interview.

Ideally, get two friends to help you: one to be the interviewer, the other to be a critic. (Do without a critic, if you must, and let the interviewer play both roles.) Use a video camera, too, if you can. It will provide an objective record of your performance that you can review several times.

Prepare your interviewer by giving her a copy of the job description. This can be the advertisement or listing you answered, if you have a copy. Also give her some background information on the company, copies of the cover letter and resume you sent to the employer, and a list of interview questions. Let the interviewer prepare any combination of questions she wants to ask, as long as she includes several tough ones.

Tips for Long-Distance Interviews

When you send your resume to an employer in response to an ad, a telephone call from the employer is the signal that you have made the first cut. The purpose of the call may be simply to schedule an in-person interview. Or the purpose may be to conduct an on-the-spot telephone interview that will qualify or disqualify you for the face-to-face meeting.

Here are some tips for handling the long-distance interview:

- Be prepared for unscheduled calls. Keep your resume and contact records within reach of the phone, along with paper and pen. Know how you'll answer tough questions. Have a prearranged signal that will tell your spouse, roommates, children, and other hangers-on that this is business and you need privacy and quiet. And always answer the phone in a businesslike manner, no matter when it rings.

- Take the call when it comes if you possibly can. Otherwise, the interviewer may skip over your name and not call back. If a call comes at a really bad time, be ready to say something like, "I'm sorry, I have an appointment in a few minutes and I want to take the time to answer your questions thoroughly. Can we reschedule for two hours from now?"

- Imagine that you are in an office or other workplace setting. This will help you get out of your informal, at-home attitude and will prevent you from being too casual with the interviewer.

- Your mission is to convince the caller by the content of what you say and by the way you say it that you merit an in-person interview. Listen for (and write down) key words in the interviewer's questions and comments, and briefly describe your relevant skills and achievements. Keep the

focus on the employer's needs and how you can meet them. Mention facts you have learned about the company through research—especially facts that are complimentary to the employer.

- Take notes that will help you further sell yourself at the face-to-face interview. Write down qualifications the interviewer stresses, challenges and concerns he describes, and so on.

- The interviewer will probably end his questioning with, "Do you have any questions?" Ask one or two questions, if you have them. But don't delay too long before saying that, from what you have learned, you are sure you can be an asset to the employer and are eager to meet. If an in-person interview hasn't yet been offered, ask for one. ("How soon can we schedule a meeting?")

- Once the interview has been agreed to, try to get some information about who will be there. Ask how long the interview will last. Be sure to ask for and write down the interviewer's exact title and the correct spelling of her name. Don't assume that "Jayne" is spelled "Jane." If the pronunciation of the name is not unmistakably clear from the spelling, write out a phonetic spelling that will remind you how to pronounce the name (for example, "Jayne Shiere [shy-AIR]"). This will save you the possible fatal embarrassment of beginning your in-person interview by mispronouncing the person's name. If you need directions to the interview site, ask whom you should contact to get them. By not asking the caller herself to give you the directions, you acknowledge the value of her time and her status in the company.

- Close by saying that you appreciate the interviewer's time and interest, and look forward to meeting him.

(See the sidebar "Turning Around Tough Questions.") Don't preview the questions; you need to practice thinking on your feet.

Begin each rehearsal with you walking into the interviewer's "office" and the two of you greeting each other. (The interviewer can vary how she gets things rolling. She may offer her hand and introduce herself first. Or she may wait for you to initiate the greeting. Practice all possible scenarios.) Have the interviewer put on a different personality each time you practice. One time she may be friendly and supportive, the next time more challenging.

Here are some things your critic should be watching for, and you should monitor if you have a videotape:

Your entrance:

- Dress and overall appearance

- Makes eye contact

- Relaxed, pleasant facial expression

- Firm handshake

- Introduction: Repeat the interviewer's name and thank her. ("It's nice to meet you, Ms. Tremaine. Thank you for the opportunity to interview for the position.")

The interview:

- Relaxed, pleasant facial expressions

- Listens attentively and doesn't interrupt

- Enthusiasm in voice, gestures, content of answers

- Appropriate body language: good posture, gestures not too stiff or extreme, no fidgeting (wringing hands, tapping foot, swinging leg, and so on)

- Maintains eye contact

- Appropriate voice: volume, tone (enthusiastic, confident); pace (too fast or slow?); no "fillers" (um)

- Complete and specific answers, not too wordy; talks about half the time

- Asks informed questions about the job when invited to do so

Your exit:

- Smiles

- Expresses enthusiasm and interest in the job

- Thanks the interviewer and says her name

Fine-Tuning Your Presentation

Don't stop rehearsing after you've had your first real interview. Each time you interview you will come away with new ideas for fine-tuning your answers and technique. Keep polishing your act.

If you've had a handful of interviews but no job offers, you may need to make some changes. It can be difficult to pinpoint what the problem is. Most experts say that when you lose out on a job, you should never ask the interviewer to critique how you did in the interview. (Although you can ask why you didn't get the job, and the answer may provide clues.) Instead, try to have someone in your industry watch you do a practice interview. Or talk through the interview experience with some people in your network, and see if they can identify a problem.

At the Interview

What to Say (and What Not to Say)

The interview starts the moment you walk through the door of the building. For all

you know, the interviewer may be the guy who rushes out of the coffee shop and into the elevator with you. If so, won't you be sorry you were putting on your lipstick during the ride?

Any last-minute grooming should be done in a restroom. (Yes, you could run into your future boss there, too. But you're in the appropriate place for applying makeup.) If you need to ask someone for directions to the office, do it in a professional manner.

Greet the secretary or receptionist with a smile and introduce yourself. Make it a point to remember her name; write it down when you can do so unobtrusively. Her opinion may very well carry some weight in the hiring decision. If you see an opportunity for a genuine compliment, give it. Don't mention anything too personal, but if there's a gorgeous bouquet on the desk, a compliment will seem natural and will be appreciated.

Don't ask for anything, including a cup of coffee, to use the phone, or anything else. A good rule of thumb is if you are offered something and want it, accept it and offer to get it yourself; if you don't, say something like, "No, thank you for asking, but I just finished a cup."

If you are kept waiting, be pleasant and patient about it. Be observant, and see what you can learn about the company and the people who work there. Check out the decor, how people greet each other, and so on. If company brochures or other materials are available, read them and, if appropriate, take them with you to review before your second interview.

Sooner or later, you will be ushered into the presence of the interviewer. (Or he will come out to meet you.) When the interviewer introduces himself, repeat his name and shake his hand. ("It's nice to meet you, Mr. Borland. Thank you for giving me the oppportunity to talk with you today.")

Be prepared to make a little small talk, but don't go on and on. Follow the interviewer's lead.

Once the interview begins in earnest, what you hear will be as important as what you say. Listen carefully to the interviewer's questions. Don't make the mistake of hearing

a buzzword or two, thinking you know what the question is going to be, and tuning out the interviewer to think about your answer. Listen attentively to the entire question, then pause briefly before you begin to answer.

Listen, too, to what the interviewer tells you about the company, the department, and the job. Be thinking about how what the interviewer is saying stacks up against your research. If there are what sound like contradictions, make a mental note to ask about them later, when the interviewer invites your questions. This is an opportunity to show off your research and your ability to think on your feet.

Finally, listen for clues about what skills and traits are most important to the employer. Emphasize those skills and traits in your answers. When the interviewer mentions a problem that needs to be solved, make sure that at some point you clearly state your ability to solve the problem. Here's an example:

> Mr. Borland, a moment ago you mentioned that you don't feel the sales training programs you've tried have been effective. As you know, I developed my own training materials for my sales staff at my last job. Sales and commissions went up. Cost of sales, turnover, and absenteeism all went down substantially. Turnover was down 40 percent, and you know how costly turnover is. The rest of the figures are in my resume. I'm confident that I can train your salespeople in a way that will yield measurable results.

Remember, the employer wants to know if you:

- Can do the job

- Can do more than the job

- Will fit in with the company's people, values, and goals

Listen for opportunities to give examples that show that you can, and you will. Present yourself as someone who will be an asset to the employer, not as someone who wants something from him. Your answers should tell, as specifically as possible, why you are the best person for the job. Explain that your skills and accomplishments are the kind the employer needs and that you are the kind of person the employer can trust to get the job done.

The interviewer is likely to begin by looking at your resume and asking you a few questions that are clearly answered there. The purpose of these questions is to make a quick check of your honesty.

You may also be asked to expand on the information in your resume. Be prepared to explain exactly how you achieved the accomplishments you have listed. For example, the interviewer may say, "Your resume says that you won three sales awards from appliance manufacturers." Answer:

> That's right. Two of the awards were for being the top salesperson in Dade County for Amalgamated Home Appliance. I received those awards in 1991 and 1992. My sales were so high because I received a very high number of referrals from my customers. I made it a point to know everything about the appliances I was selling. I educated my customers about all the different things you have to consider when making a purchase. I also gave them copies of articles from the top two consumer magazines, showing that Amalgamated Appliances were ranked Number One for value. The third award was from Acme Appliance, in 1994. I was their top salesperson in South Florida. I used similar selling methods that year too, and again I got many referrals.

When It's Your Turn to Ask the Questions

When the interviewer has asked all the questions she wants to ask you, she will toss the ball into your court, giving you an opportunity to question her. Your questions must be informed questions,

TELL 'EM YOUR P.P.S.

When an interviewer asks you why you want to work for her company, why she should hire you, or what you have to offer, your p.p.s. may be the perfect answer.

The interviewer isn't familiar with the term "p.p.s.," so leave off the label and present your p.p.s. as a normal part of the conversation. But your p.p.s. **is** a short, high-impact statement of why you are the right person for the job, and mentioning its contents will be helpful.

Turning Around Tough Questions

They're the questions you dread. The ones about all the job changing early in your career and those long months of unemployment back in 1991. How are you ever going to explain that stuff? We're about to tell you how. Here, four all-too-common tough questions, what they really mean, and how to answer them.

The Question: "Why did you leave your last job?"

The questions behind the question: "Were you fired? Are you too demanding? Do you have trouble getting along with people? Do you blame your problems on other people?"

The answer: The best answer is always the truth, conveyed in a brief and straightforward fashion that will reassure the interviewer that you are easy to get along with, good-natured, and willing to take responsibility for your own life and your own problems. You don't actually have to go into tons of detail about why you left your last job, you just have to give an answer. No matter what went on at your last job or how you felt about it, you must not say anything negative about your previous employer or anyone you worked with. What you can say is: "I wanted to be in a position to make a greater contribution." "I wanted more challenge." "I wanted a smaller, faster-growing company." "I wanted an opportunity to take on more responsibility."

The Question: "I notice you were unemployed for nearly a year before your last job. Why was that?"

The questions behind the question: "Is there something wrong with you that we haven't noticed yet? Are you lazy?"

The answer: Don't blame it on the economy, even if you did find your-self job-hunting during a recession that hit your industry hard. Focus your answer on what you accomplished while you weren't working. "It was

during that time that I studied for and passed the C.P.A. exam." Talk about a career-related accomplishment if you can. But a significant personal commitment may also turn what appears to be a negative into a positive. "I spent the year tutoring underprivileged kids."

The Question: "Why have you moved around so much in your career?"

The questions behind the question: "Are you unstable? Have you been fired several times?"

The answer: If you did your job-hopping years ago, say you tried on several careers and found the right one for you. If you consistently moved up to positions of greater responsibility, point this out. If you moved because you were repeatedly offered more money and more opportunity, say so. If you used the same skills at all your various jobs, point out the consistency beneath the apparent inconsistency. Conversely, you may be asked why you stayed in a position so long. In this case, point out how the job developed over time, even if your job title did not.

The Question: "What do you feel is your biggest weakness?"

The questions behind the question: "Is there some part of this job that you will be unable to do? Are you an egomaniac who is unable to admit that you have weaknesses?"

The answer: You must say something, of course. But it must be something safe—something that couldn't possibly affect your suitability for the job (or for later promotions). You can go one of two ways. You can name a "weakness" that everybody knows is really a strength: "I get impatient with people who come in late or miss a lot of workdays. I put in my time, and I think other people should, too." Or you can tell about a weakness you used to have and how you overcame it: "For a long time, I didn't feel comfortable asking for help on the job. I felt that I should be able to do it all. I'd struggle along on my own and, frankly, sometimes things took me longer than they should have. My last boss helped me realize that there's a learning process in any job—that it's okay if you don't always know how to do everything, as long as you're willing to learn."

not general questions that should have been answered by your preinterview research. Some possibilities:

- Is this a newly created position, or has it existed for some time? (If it is an existing position, you can ask why it is open and where the person who held it last is now.)

- Who is the immediate supervisor for the job?

- How, and how often, is job performance evaluated?

- What kind of career path could the person in this job expect? What kinds of future opportunities might be available?

- If it has not been made clear what the most important duties and responsibilities of the job are, and how the job relates to the company's activities and goals, now is the time to clarify.

- If it has not been clear what the next step in the hiring process will be (another round of interviews, or a decision?), now is the time to ask.

Some things you should be careful not to do:

- Don't interrupt the interviewer, whether he is asking a question, explaining something, or rattling on about the weather. He is in charge; he gets to talk as much as he wants.

- Don't be suckered into bad-mouthing your previous employers, your potential employer's competition, or anyone else. And don't blame others for your failures.

- Don't monopolize the conversation. Studies show that successful interviewees do only about half the talking.

- Don't ramble. Studies also show that your answers should take 20 seconds to 2 minutes, rarely longer. Your answers must be focused, giving relevant details and leaving out the rest.

- Don't, on the other hand, answer "yes" or "no" and stop there. Expand your answer by explaining "how" or "why."

- Don't pretend to understand a word you don't understand, or to know someone you don't know. Even at the risk of sounding dumb, if you don't understand something the interviewer says, say so. It's honest, it will prevent you from being exposed later, and it shows that you're willing to acknowledge your weaknesses.

- Don't say something—anything!—to fill an uncomfortable silence. If the interviewer at some point just sits there looking at you, keep a pleasant expression and look back. The interviewer may be testing you to see what you'll do (will you let him be in charge, or will you take over for him?) or if you'll blurt out something silly. Or he may be thinking about whether to offer you the job.

- Don't ask any questions about what's in it for you. It is not appropriate to bring up salary, benefits, or anything about what the employer can do for you.

There's a second kind of question that you should be prepared to ask in an interview, and ask often. Qualifying questions. These are questions you ask in response to your interviewer's questions so that you can be sure you are giving her the most clued-in answer possible. All too often, interviewees jump to conclusions about a question and then go on a long tirade about something unrelated. You should almost always work to clarify questions when they're asked. Some examples of qualifying questions:

- "Is that important here?"

- "Has that been an area where you've had trouble before?"

- "What sort of impact can I have on your organization?"

- "Can you tell me more about that?"

- "Is this something new here?"

- "Are you generally pleased with the way _____ is progressing?"

- "What sort of changes have you made recently?"

What specific qualifying questions you ask will depend on what you are asked. There are four (!) reasons to ask questions like this:

1. It gives your subconscious mind more time to form a response.

2. It shows interest on your part in what the interviewer is getting at.

3. It makes it more likely you understand the real reason behind the question.

4. It gives the interviewer a chance to hear his favorite sound, his own voice.

These questions may also help you uncover all sorts of interesting insights.

When You Meet the Whole Crew

After the interview, you may be asked to meet with various other people, from other managers to the people who will be your coworkers if you are hired. This is a good sign. You are being given serious consideration, or the interviewer wouldn't waste these people's time by asking them to meet you.

Treat these introductions as informal interviews. The people you meet might have a say in the hiring decision.

If the interviewer stays with you, the introductions are intended to be very brief. You may make a bit of small talk or ask a question or two about the person's job before moving on. If the interviewer leaves you with another employee, it's because he is someone you would work closely with. The two of you are being asked to size each other up, to decide if you would work well together. Feel free to ask questions that will fill in any blanks you have about the job or the company. Ask how long the person has been with the company, what different jobs he has done, and how he likes his current job. This will give you a clue to whether the company promotes from within and whether a clear career path exists. Expect to hear positive things. (If you don't, beware. An employee who is willing to gripe to someone who may report back to his boss is a very unhappy employee.) Listen to the tone of the answers you get, as much as to the content.

The Interviewer Who Doesn't

Oddly enough, the most difficult kind of interview may be the kind where the interviewer doesn't get around to interviewing you. Instead, she talks about the weather, her last vacation, the company picnic, her dog, her mother-in-law, and pretty much everything except the business at hand. She's not prepared and she's not focused.

To salvage this kind of interview, you'll need to create opportunities to talk about your strengths, and then make the most of them. One tactic is to wait until the interviewer has to pause for breath, then ask a focused question about the job to try to get things on track. ("What do you see as the most difficult aspect of this job?") You're allowing the interviewer to do what she wants to do (talk), but getting her to talk about the job.

Then, at every pause, make a brief, pointed statement about your abilities.

It may be as simple as saying, "I can do that." No matter how much the interviewer is boring or irritating you, be attentive and enthusiastic—especially if you want the job. Nod, smile, agree. Many of your competitors for the job have probably yawned, rolled their eyes, or tried to take over the conversation. In short, they have reminded the interviewer of her incompetence. She is likely to hire the person who makes her feel good about herself.

Be pleasant, enthusiastic, and professional with everyone you meet. Take every opportunity to show that you would fit in well, if you think you would. If you are introduced to a group of employees on their break who are talking about the company softball team, let them know that you played shortstop on your last company's team and can't wait to get back on the field.

Sometimes you will meet your prospective coworkers first, before interviewing with your potential boss. This probably means that the crew's opinion of you will carry a lot of weight in the hiring decision.

How to Excel at the Second Interview

What the second interview is all about depends entirely on the employer. When you are invited to a second interview, it almost always means one of the following:

- You did well in the preliminary interview and are now part of a smaller pool of candidates who are still being considered. In this scenario, the first interview was probably with someone in the Human Resources department, or someone who works for the manager who will actually make the hire. The second interview will be with the person doing the hiring. It will be the decision-making interview.

- You are a candidate of choice, but the choice must be confirmed by the person you will see in the second interview. In this case, the first interview was most likely with the person who will make the offer. (Often, it is the same person who will be your boss.) But before that happens, you must win the approval of the second interviewer. This may be the first interviewer's boss, or some other manager who will be affected by the hiring decision.

- You are one of two or more candidates who performed very well in the first interview and are in a neck-and-neck race for the job. If you are interviewed a second time by the same person, this is probably what's going on.

What You Must Do in the Second Interview

When you receive an invitation to a second interview, first say how happy you are. Then, do some gentle (not pushy) probing to find out as much as you can about what you're in for. Try to establish which of the scenarios just mentioned is playing out. At the very least, it is certainly reasonable for you to ask for the name and title of the person with whom you will be interviewing, and whether that person would be your supervisor if you were hired.

Handling Illegal Questions

Questions about your race and ethnic background, age, and religion are illegal under federal law. State laws vary, but most states forbid questions about your personal life (such as your marital status, whether you have and/or plan to have children, what your child-care arrangements are). It is legal for an employer to ask if you have been convicted of a crime, but not if you have been arrested or have had a problem with alcohol or drug abuse.

Some interviewers try to camouflage questions they're not supposed to ask, hoping to get the information they want without you realizing what they're asking. Or the question may not be a question at all, but a leading statement.

For example, an interviewer may say to a female candidate, "I see you're wearing a wedding ring. I bet you're very family-oriented." The unspoken questions are: Do you have children? Are you planning to have children? You're perfectly free, of course, to leave the answers unspoken as well. Ignore the statement and turn the conversation back to business.

When an interviewer asks you a question that you know is illegal, you have a decision to make. You can choose to answer the question, especially if you really want the job and don't think your answer will hurt your chances. Equal-opportunity employment laws were designed to defend the particularly downtrodden from the particularly egregious. Most workplaces aren't so bad, and your situation might not be so bad either. In other words, people want to work with people who are fun to work with. If you are sending off legal radar signals from the very first question, there is no reason to suspect you will be hired. The interviewer may assume you are a troublemaker. You can say something like, "How would that affect my work?" Say it with a smile, and the interviewer will probably just move on.

Or if you honestly feel that the interviewer is out of line, you can say that the question is illegal and that you intend to file a formal complaint with the federal Equal Employment Opportunity Commission or your state's commission. The employer may be cowed into offering you a job on the spot, to avoid trouble. But a working relationship based on a threat is hardly ideal. Besides, an employer who asks illegal questions in an interview may very well engage in other illegal and/or unethical activities.

Because every company and every hiring decision is different, it is difficult to make generalizations about second interviews. That said, let's look back at the three things employers need to know about you in order to hire you. They need to know that you:

• Can do the job

• Can do more than the job

• Will fit in with the company's people, values, and goals

Generally speaking, you can assume you convinced the first interviewer that you can do the job. That's what got you invited back. The second interview is partly about confirming that you are the kind of person who will do the job, and mostly about deciding whether you really will fit in.

Be alert to clues during the interview that will tell you whether this generalization is true in your case. If the interviewer asks you to confirm some things you said in the first interview and then escorts you around the company to introduce you to everybody, the primary purpose of the interview is to see how you fit in.

However, if the interviewer asks some of the same tough questions you answered in the first round, or asks even more detailed questions, the employer may still have some uncertainty about your ability to do the job. It is likely that there are other candidates

How to Excuse Yourself If You Know the Fit's Not Right

Here's an embarrassing situation: You researched the company, you went after the job, you got the interview, you're sitting there across from your would-be future boss, and your brain is screaming: "Run away! Run away!"

Maybe you knew the minute you walked into the grimy, stale-smelling office with the cigarette burns in the gray indoor-outdoor carpet and the teetering stacks of papers everywhere. Gee, you were thinking, it doesn't look anything like the photos on the Web site. But then, that was company headquarters, and this is "the annex."

Or maybe you didn't really know for sure until your would-be future boss, the assistant vice president of industrial operations, walked in wearing a sort of industrial-looking muumuu. Maybe it was her burnt-orange hair, or the way her cigarette jerked in her mouth when she talked—the amazingly long ash miraculously clinging to the end.

Or maybe it was the way she scratched the back of her head when she said, "You can see we need some help around here, huh, honey?"

Whatever it was, something turned you off about this job, and you just want to go home. How do you bow out gracefully?

Don't worry, it's easy. You just say, "I'm very sorry to have taken your time. I'm afraid I just wouldn't fit in here." Remember, one of the employer's three big questions about you is, "Will this person fit in?" If you come right out and say that you won't, that should pretty much end her interest.

If the red lights are less glaring than the ones just described, you may want to be more diplomatic. If there has been a misunderstanding about the job, you can say so gently. ("I'm sorry to have taken your

time. I understood that the job was here in Springfield. I'm not able to commute to Summerville.") But if it's just not a fit, you may want to endure the interview graciously and decline the second interview or job offer if one is made.

Be polite, remembering that the interviewer may someday be in a position to recommend you for a job that is right for you.

who also have very strong skills and impressive accomplishments. The employer is trying to decide who is the one best candidate among several excellent contenders. You must emphasize any unique skills, experiences, and accomplishments you can bring to the job—anything you can offer that other candidates cannot. You must present yourself as the person who can solve the employer's biggest problem and add the most value. Demonstrate your knowledge of the company and show real enthusiasm for making a specific, substantial contribution.

When You Are Offered a Job

Even if you were told the interview was a preliminary meeting, there is a chance that you will be offered a job at the end of your first interview. Of course, there is an even better chance of an offer at the end of a second interview. You should always be prepared for this happy eventuality.

When an offer is made, respond with appreciation and enthusiasm. Say something like, "I'm very enthusiastic about this company and this position. I know I can make an important contribution here, and I'd be very happy to discuss the details of an offer."

The interviewer should be prepared to give you the details of the salary and benefits being offered. If he is not, consider the offer tentative, not a firm offer. Don't suspend your other job-hunting activities, and by all means don't give notice to your current

employer. You don't have a real offer until you know exactly what you're being offered.

Assuming, though, that the interviewer makes a detailed offer, it is reasonable for you to ask for a minimum of two to three days and a maximum of a week to make a decision. (If taking the job would require a long-distance move or some other major lifestyle change, a week is justified.) And assuming you are interested in the job, you will use the time to think over the compensation package you are being offered and to prepare to negotiate the best deal you can get.

If you are offered a job and then pressured to give your decision on the spot, be very suspicious. There's usually something wrong when this happens—something the company doesn't want you to have time to find out. Insist on taking at least 24 hours to consider the offer (and to try to figure out what's wrong). You're not likely to lose the job over such a reasonable request. If you do, chances are it's no great loss.

Checking Out the Benefits

When you are offered a job, checking out the benefits is as important as evaluating the salary. Benefits comprise about 20 to

"IT'S NOT YOUR FAULT"

There's something about a job interview that makes you feel like a kid again. A kid in the principal's office, that is. The other person has power and authority (in this case, to hire you or not). You don't. She is confident and in charge. You're not. The situation is stressful under the best of circumstances. If you have the bad luck to encounter the kind of interviewer who spent her childhood pulling the wings off flies, it can temporarily destroy your self-esteem.

You walk in the door with the attitude that the person across the desk from you is someone who is worthy of your respect. If that person proceeds to berate you, or use four-letter words, or raise her voice, it's probably going to shake you up. Your first reaction probably will be, "Oh my gosh, I blew it! I said something stupid! I made her mad!" If this happens to you, you must repeat these magic words until your heart rate returns to normal:

"It's not my fault. It's not my fault." It's not your fault. There's no excuse for such behavior, no matter what you said.

The problem is, you got a jerk for an interviewer. And you wouldn't work for somebody like her for a million bucks. Would you?

40 percent of the total compensation for most jobs. You need to know exactly what benefits you will be getting.

Unless the person making the offer is a Human Resources professional, he may not understand all the details of the benefits package himself. Ask if there's someone in Human Resources that you can talk to. Most companies, unless they are very small, have benefits specialists. Ask for written information about benefits, especially health care and pension benefits, which can be complex.

Here is a list of the most commonly offered benefits. When considering whether to accept a job offer and how to negotiate your compensation, think about which benefits are most important to you.

• Health insurance

• Life insurance

• Disability insurance

• Maternity/paternity leave

• Pension plans and/or 401(k) plans (the latter are essentially pension plans to which you contribute)

• Profit-sharing plans

• Stock options

• Paid vacations

• Paid sick leave

• Employer-paid expenses: car, gas, professional memberships and subscriptions, educational fees and tuition, and so on

• Expense accounts for business-related entertaining and other expenses

• Child care (provided or paid for by the employer)

- Employee assistance programs (psychological counseling, stop-smoking programs, health club facilities, and so on)

- Flexible hours

- Compensation days (time off to compensate for overtime)

- Work-at-home options

- Bonuses, usually based on individual or company performance

Important questions to ask about health care benefits include:

- Will your insurance cover any preexisting conditions that you or members of your family have?

- Are dental care and optical services covered?

- When does coverage begin? Usually there is a waiting period after you are hired. During this period, you will need to have other insurance.

- What is the cost to you of the insurance; i.e., what is your share of the premium cost?

- What are the deductible amounts; i.e., how much do you have to pay for services each year before the insurance begins paying?

- What percentage of costs does the insurance pay after you have met the deductibles?

- What are the caps, or maximum amounts, that the insurance will pay?

Talking about Money

Answering questions about your former salary and negotiating your future salary can be tricky. There are two things that will give you an advantage and help you get the best possible deal. First, be informed. Do your research on salary so that you're ready

to negotiate with facts and figures, not emotional pleas. Second, know what questions you'll be asked and how to answer them to your benefit.

Some salary questions you may be asked, and how to answer them:

"What is your salary history?"

The question means, "Have you received consistent, substantial raises over the years?" The interviewer is probing to see how well you've done in your current employer's eyes and how well you've been rewarded. Have you moved up steadily, or have you been stuck at one salary level?

Answer: "My salary increased consistently." (Assuming this is true.) This doesn't necessarily mean that you received every raise you asked for or were eligible for, but that there has been an upward trend to your salary.

If the interviewer presses for specifics of the dates and amounts of your raises (which is unlikely), say you would need to check your records for this information. Then wait to see if the interviewer asks you to do so. She probably won't, but if she does, you will have to agree. Still, don't offer the details unless you're asked again (which is even more unlikely).

If you have to come through with the numbers and your raises weren't impressive, explain why. Maybe there was a freeze on raises, or maybe you were offered other perks, such as a cut in hours, instead of cash. However, if less-than-adequate raises contributed to your leaving the job, say so.

"How much are you making now?"

Answer: Tell the truth. Don't lie about your salary; you are almost certain to be found out. Your prospective employer can make the job offer contingent on salary verification. He can then ask you to bring in a payroll stub or request salary verification directly from your last employer. He needs your written permission to do this, but, again, you don't have much choice except to give it.

"What salary do you require?"

(Of course, this question may be stated in any number of different ways. Regardless of the exact words that are used, the question comes down to, "How much do you want?")

Answer: Review for the interviewer the job requirements and duties you have discussed, ask if you have stated them correctly. Then ask, "What does the company normally pay for such a position?" Or, "What would be the normal range for someone who brings my skills and accomplishments to the job?" Try to get the interviewer to give a figure first.

If you must give a figure, you'll be glad you did your research. You know the low, average, and high salary ranges for the job, and you can say so. If you have been able to find out how much the employer you're talking to pays others who are doing the job, that's even better. Don't come right out and say that you have this information, though. Just give the range that you know the company is paying. Then say something like, "With my skills and achievements, I think my salary should be on the high end of this range. Do you agree?"

Another tack is to give a range that starts higher than their bottom and ends higher than their top. For example, if you know the company pays between $35,000 and $38,000 for this job, say that your acceptable range would be $37,000 to $40,000. Again, make your case that your salary should be at the high end of the range.

If you aren't asked about salary, but instead are offered a figure, you'll still want to negotiate.

If the offer is less than you are making now (or were making at your last job), say so. Make your case for more, using the research you have done. For example, if the offer is low by industry standards, give some figures and tell where you got them. Emphasize any way in which your skills, experience, and accomplishments make you especially valuable to the employer. Never talk about your needs; always talk about your value to the employer.

If the offer just matches what you made at your last job, point out any additional

duties or increased responsibilities in the job you are being offered. If your last job offered exceptionally good benefits (i.e., better than those at the new job), point out that they added value to your former compensation package.

If the offer is more than you made at your last job but you think it should be even higher, be ready to justify the request with facts.

When you want the job but are having trouble agreeing on a salary, here are two ways to make the deal work:

- Try to negotiate additional benefits in lieu of more money. Look over the benefits listed earlier. Decide which ones you would like to have added to your compensation package, and ask if the employer is willing. Some benefits cost the employer less than cash but may mean just as much to you. Flexible hours and work-at-home options are two common examples. These benefits often cost the employer virtually nothing and may save you money in child care, commuting expense, and so on.

- Agree to the starting salary the employer is offering, with the provision that you will get a raise to your requested salary after a set period of time (usually three months or six months). The raise may be pegged to your meeting or exceeding certain performance standards. A similar tactic is to ask for a bonus at the end of the first year that will bring your total salary up to the level you are requesting. The employer gets to hold onto the extra money until you prove yourself worthy of it.

How to Say Good-Bye

When the interviewer signals that the meeting is over, continue to be upbeat and enthusiastic, no matter where things stand. If you haven't received an offer or an invitation to another interview, say that you are very interested in the job (if you are). Ask for clarification about what will happen next. Put your question in positive terms: "When can I expect to hear from you about the next step?"

Never try to force the interviewer's hand by mentioning other job possibilities you have. (Only if you have a firm job offer—in writing—from another company should you mention it. In this case, you have real leverage; you're in a position to take whichever offer stacks up best. But if the other offer is not in writing, keep mum. See "Accepting the Job and Confirming the Details," following.) On the flip side, no matter how badly you would like to hear an offer at this point, don't grovel. Be professional. End the meeting as you began it, with a firm handshake, eye contact, and a thank-you, using the interviewer's name.

After the Interview

Don't blow a perfect interview by faltering at the final stretch. By observing a few simple rules, you enhance your chances of making a good impression.

Thank-Yous and Following Up

The day after your interview, send the interviewer a thank-you letter.

This is one area of business communication where an old-fashioned, snail-mailed letter is still preferred to faxes and e-mails. If you were interviewed by more than one person, address the letter only to the main interviewer. If you are not absolutely positive of the correct spelling of his name and his correct job title, call an administrative assistant or the Human Resources department to confirm them.

Keep your letter to one page; three or four paragraphs is all it should take.

Here's what your thank-you letter should do:

- First, thank the interviewer for his interest and time. Give him some information that will remind him which candidate you are, such as: "Thank you for giving me the opportunity to interview with you Thursday afternoon for the administrative assistant position. I enjoyed talking with you about the company's plans for expansion in my hometown, Akron."

- Mention anything important about your qualifications that you forgot to mention in the interview or that you want to emphasize. Example: "As I mentioned when we talked, in my last job I established a company record for on-time distribution of financial statements. I am confident that I can

solve your recurring problem of late statements and consistently deliver them on time."

• Express your enthusiastic interest in the job and say that you are looking forward to talking further with him.

If, after a week, you haven't heard from the employer, it's time to call (unless you have been told that a decision will take longer). It's possible that candidates are still being interviewed, that the interviewer is out sick, or any number of things. But it's also possible that you'll get bad news: You didn't get the job.

If you didn't get the job, politely ask why. The answer may tell you that there is nothing you could have done differently. (For example, the winning candidate may have been a former employee of the company who was known and loved by all.) Or it may tell you something that will be helpful to you in future interviews. One job seeker who had recently moved from the West Coast to the Midwest got the bad news from a secretary who was kind enough to tell her what the problem was: "The executives weren't comfortable with your hair color." Yes, it's a dumb reason to not hire someone. But there's no law against hair-color prejudice. The executives felt that the woman, a peroxide blonde, did not fit in. Her next "interview" was at a local hair salon.

Accepting the Job and Confirming the Details

Of course, sooner or later, you'll hear the words you've been waiting to hear: They want you.

It is most likely that the initial job offer will be made verbally, either in person or over the phone. Until the offer is in writing, don't stake your career on it. All kinds of things can happen to derail your new job, some of which have nothing to do with you or with your new employer's integrity. A manager may make you an offer one day and learn the next day that the job has been cut from her budget. Or imagine this: The person who offered you a job goes back to his office after your interview and finds a pink slip on his desk. In his distress, he packs up and leaves without ever telling anyone he made you an offer. When you show up for work three weeks later, his replacement tells you that she just hired someone else to do "your" job. Stranger things have happened.

Don't breathe a word of your intentions to your current employer until you have a written offer of employment from the new company. And while you may reasonably slow down your job hunt, don't bring everything to a screeching halt. If you have told other employers that you would follow up with them, do it. Keep your commitments and your options open.

When the offer is made verbally, accept verbally, confirming all important elements of the offer (salary, benefits, starting date). Say that you are very happy to be coming to work for the company and look forward to getting started. Then say something like, "I need to give my current employer two weeks' notice. So, in order to start with you on the fifteenth, I will need to receive your written offer no later than the first." Make sure the written offer includes all the details you and the employer agreed on, including your salary and benefits. If the employer agreed to any special provisions, such as a raise after 90 days contingent on your performance, make sure this is in the written offer.

Respond with a written acceptance that refers to the offer letter (so it will be clear what you are accepting) and confirms your starting date. Then, and only then, give notice to your current employer. Send letters to any other employers you have been talking with, letting them know about your new job and thanking them for their interest in you.

YOU'RE hired! Making the right FIRST MOVES

CHAPTER NINE

*You've arrived. You've got the job you wanted, the job you **envisioned** when your wrote your p.p.s., the job you worked hard to get. **Congratulations!***

Now all you have to do is learn a new job, get to know a whole new corporate culture, figure out a whole bunch of new people, and remain calm, cool, and collected while you're doing it! In this chapter you'll find some strategies to help you succeed.

What Now?

For the first few months, make like a sponge: absorb. You'll work hard at your job, of course, and master it as quickly as you can. But at the same time, keep your eyes and ears open to everything that's going on around you.

Imagine that you have just arrived in a foreign country, and you need to learn the local culture so you can blend in. Pay attention to how people dress (just how casual is casu-

al Friday?) and how they talk (how do they address one another? what slang do they use? what buzzwords do you hear over and over? what words do you not hear?).

Know the organizational chart for the company and for your department. Scope out the photos in the company newsletter and learn who's who. If the CEO gets on the elevator with you, you should be able to greet her by name and introduce yourself.

But go beyond the official hierarchy and learn who the movers and shakers are. Watch and listen for clues about who is in favor with top management and moving up through the ranks, who is not, and why. Pay attention to who comes in early, stays late, works weekends, and takes work home. Make a mental note of alliances and feuds; know who gets along and who doesn't. Don't get involved, just get informed.

Make it a point to meet and talk with many of your coworkers in different departments and at different levels of the organization. Don't pair off with the first person you meet. You want to get as many different perspectives on the company as you can. Ask people to lunch, one or two at a time. Get involved in company social activities, such as athletic teams. If everyone in your department heads off to the lounge for a lunchtime going-away party for a fellow employee you haven't even met, go and be friendly. Don't give anyone an excuse to label you a loner or a party pooper. Instead, build a network that will, over time, provide you with the support and information that you will need to succeed. When new problems arise, or when plans, priorities, and goals change, there won't always be an official announcement. It's up to you stay clued in and to respond to changing realities.

Adapt to what you learn. Don't say, "This isn't the way we did it where I used to work." Learn how they do it here, and jump in.

Keep a Journal

You'll have a lot to think about in your first few months on a new job. While you're getting to know the corporate culture and who's who, you also have a job to do. And with so much on your mind, it can be easy to lose track of just how you're doing.

To stay focused, keep a journal of your significant achievements, frustrations, and mistakes. (Yes, there will be mistakes.) For most people, once-a-week entries are suffi-

cient. On Friday evening or first thing Saturday morning, write an entry for the previous week. You'll have enough perspective to separate the trivial from the important, but you'll still be close enough to the events to remember them in detail.

Describe anything significant that happened during the week. Include things such as meeting a goal or deadline, learning a new process, miscommunicating with your boss or a coworker, or missing a meeting because you didn't know about it.

In addition to logging the events themselves, write down your feelings, reflections, insights, and interpretations. Add notes about things like what caused a mistake, how you can prevent it from happening again, who helped you undo the damage, and so on. Be sure to date your entries.

You'll gain insight just from putting things on paper and looking at them in black and white. You'll also be able to look back and identify patterns, recurrent problems, areas where you're performing especially well, and so on. This information will help you resolve difficulties and build on your strengths.

Review your journal just before your performance evaluation, and you'll be able to talk specifically with your boss about how you're doing. If you disagree with her assessment of any aspect of your performance, you'll be able to make your case with specifics.

Finally, the next time you rewrite your resume you can mine your journal for accomplishments to include.

Keep your journal at home, away from prying eyes. But do keep it.

What Next?

Always be thinking about your career path and what might be next for you. Stay informed about problems, plans, priorities, and changes in the company as a whole and in your department. Read in-house publications (employee newsletters and so on), trade publications, and media coverage of the company. Listen to what your fellow employees are saying. Each time you encounter news, ask yourself: How might this affect my job, my career? What new challenges might there be? What opportunities? What new skills might I need? Look ahead, and be prepared.

Building Skills

One of the best ways to be prepared for the changes that are sure to come is to continue building your skills. Look for opportunities to further develop skills you already have. This might mean asking for an assignment that will allow you to stretch your wings. Or it might mean taking courses or even earning a degree.

In addition, add new skills that will make you even more valuable in tomorrow's workplace. Look at the problems your company or your industry is facing, and figure out what skills will be needed to solve them. Then go after those skills. Look at your company's plans for the future, and make sure you're ready to make a contribution to them. For example, if your company has big plans to expand into Latin America, you might learn Spanish and take courses in Latin American politics and economics.

If you're like most people, you want to make more money as you get older and acquire more experience. But it won't happen automatically. You'll need to contribute more in order to earn more.

WHAT'S GOING ON IN THE OUTSIDE WORLD?

Stay informed about what's happening in the world outside your company's walls. Changes in the economy and in your industry will affect your company and your job. Is new competition on the way? New technology? New regulation? Again, the key is to be prepared.

Keeping in Touch with Old Friends

Once you're working again, stay in touch with your network. As soon as you can, get in touch with all the people you contacted during your job search. Thank them again for their help. Let them know where you are, how you got there, and how they contributed. Encourage them to keep in touch with you and to call on you if there's some way you can return the favor they have done you.

If appropriate, include in your network coworkers at your former job. They can be a good source of information about your industry.

Make a Date with Yourself for a Checkup

When you start your new job, flip forward six months in your daily planner and schedule a career checkup for yourself. When the day of your checkup arrives, ask yourself these questions:

- Is this the right job for me? Am I performing well and feeling satisfied? What weaknesses or problems do I need to address? (Review your journal.)

- Is this the right company for me? Do I fit in?

- Am I building a network for support and information?

- What changes are occurring or about to occur (both inside the company and outside), and how will they affect me? How do I need to respond to these changes?

- Do I see opportunities for the kind of future I want? How can I prepare to take advantage of those opportunities?

You may want to be proactive and schedule an informal review with your employer at this time.

It's a good idea to do this same checkup again at one year and at least once a year thereafter.

Postscript: What Ever Happened to Jonathan?

You remember Jonathan. First he created his p.p.s.: "I am an informal person who excels at learning how to use new technologies and helping others to understand and use them."

Next, he researched some industries to figure out where he would fit.

He networked his way to a job interview with a telecommunications company.

He did his preinterview research and impressed the interviewer so much that he got the job.

End of story? Nope. It gets better.

When Jonathan was hired, he was told that because the company was expanding quickly, he would be eligible for a promotion after one year if he did well. He was assured that hard work would be rewarded with opportunities to make a good career with the company.

Doing well came easily, because Jonathan loved the job. He had a rare ability to calm down upset customers, and he never lost his patience. He was able to explain technical problems and solutions in terms his customers understood. Within weeks, two of Jonathan's coworkers who were struggling came to him for help. Often, Jonathan came in a few minutes early or stayed a few minutes late to listen to their frustrations and suggest ways to deal with irate customers. Jonathan's supervisor noticed. One of the grateful coworkers told the supervisor that she would have quit in frustration if it hadn't been for Jonathan.

One day at lunch, Jonathan overheard two of the other supervisors talking about the need for a department newsletter. The company didn't have a publications department; they would need to find some volunteers in their own department to create and publish the newsletter. Jonathan introduced himself and explained that he knew how to create newsletters using page layout software. He'd be happy to produce one for the department if they could round up some writers. Six weeks later, the first issue was distributed to all the company's customer-care employees.

After four months on the job, Jonathan was called into his supervisor's office. He was a little nervous, because usually she just approached him at his desk when she needed to talk with him.

It was nothing to be nervous about. Jonathan was getting a promotion and a raise. His duties really wouldn't change, but he would move up one number in the company's formal ranking system. And the raise was substantial. The supervisor said this was in recognition of the extra effort Jonathan was making with his customers and his coworkers.

Three months later, Jonathan's supervisor asked if he would be willing to take some tests. They would be similar to the skills and personality tests he took when he was hired, she said, but a bit more advanced. Jonathan agreed.

His boss didn't explain the purpose of the testing until the results came back. Two more supervisors were needed, she said. Jonathan's test results qualified him for the move up. If he was interested, he could interview with the vice president.

The following week, Jonathan interviewed for and was offered a supervisor's position. His new salary was nearly double what he had started at less than eight months before. According to formal company policy, Jonathan wasn't even eligible for a first promotion for another four months. But the company was happy to bend policy and give Jonathan an opportunity to make a greater contribution—an opportunity management knew he would make the most of, to everyone's benefit.

Jonathan's experience is a good example of what can happen when a job seeker identifies the job that is really right for him and goes after it. Jonathan enjoys the job he does all day, because he gets to be himself and use his most outstanding skills. That makes it easy to work hard and stay motivated. He keeps finding new ways to contribute to his department and to the company's goals. As a result, he is being recognized and rewarded with steadily increasing responsibility, status, and salary.

By now you've learned the key elements for a successful job search. You've learned how to be committed, you understand the art of networking, and you've mastered the art of nailing the interview. Wherever you are in your job search, if you're being guided by your p.p.s. and using the information in this book, you're on your way to your own happy ending: the beginning of a new job, or a whole new career, that is right for you.

RESOURCES

Books

50 Ways to Get Hired. Max Messmer (William Morrow & Co., 1994).

100 Best Careers for the 21st Century. Shelly Field (Arco Publishing, 1996).

101 Dynamite Questions to Ask at Your Job Interview. Richard Fein (Impact Publications, 1996).

101 Great Answers to the Toughest Job Search Problems. Ollie Stevenson (Career Press, 1995).

101 Ways to Power Up Your Job Search. J. Thomas Buck, William R. Matthews, and Robert N. Leech (McGraw-Hill, 1997).

175 High-Impact Cover Letters. Richard H. Beatty (John Wiley & Sons, 1996).

200 Letters for Job Hunters. William S. Frank (Ten Speed Press, 1993).

201 Dynamite Job Search Letters. Ronald L. Krannich, Caryl Rae Krannich, and Ron Krannich (Impact Publications, 1997).

201 Killer Cover Letters. Sandra Podesta and Andrea Paxton (McGraw-Hill, 1996).

The 1998 What Color Is Your Parachute: A Practical Manual for Job-Hunters and Career Changers. Richard Nelson Bolles (Ten Speed Press, 1997).

The Adams Cover Letter Almanac. Robert L. Adams, editor (Adams Publishing, 1995).

Adams Electronic Job Search Almanac 1997. Emily E. Ehrenstein, editor (Adams Publishing, 1997).

Adams Job Interview Almanac and CD–ROM. (Adams Publishing, 1997).

The American Almanac of Jobs and Salaries 1997–1998. John W. Wright (Avon Books, 1996).

Ask the Headhunter: Reinventing the Interview to Win the Job. Nick A. Corcodilos (Plume, 1997).

Best Answers to the 201 Most Frequently Asked Interview Questions. Matthew J. Deluca (McGraw-Hill, 1996).

The Big Book of Jobs. Barbara Spencer Hawk, editor (VGM Career Horizons, 1996).

Career Development by Design. Sharon L. Hanna (Prentice Hall, 1997).

Career Focus: A Personal Job Search Guide. Helene Martucci Lamarre (Prentice Hall, 1997).

Careerxroads: The 1998 Directory to Jobs, Resumes and Career Management on the World Wide Web. Gerry Crispin and Mark Mehler (IEEE, 1997).

Coming Alive from Nine to Five: The Career Search Handbook. Betty Neville Michelozzi (Mayfield Publishing Co., 1996).

The Complete Job Search Organizer 1997–98: How to Get a Great Job—Fast. Jack O'Brien (Times Books, 1997).

Discover the Best Jobs for You! Find the Job to Get a Life You Love. Ronald L. Krannich, Caryl Rae Krannich, and Ron Krannich (Impact Publications, 1997).

Do What You Are: Discover the Perfect Career for You through the Secrets of Personality Type. Paul D. Tieger and Barbara Barron-Tieger (Little Brown, 1995).

Dynamite Answers to Interview Questions; No More Sweaty Palms! Caryl Rae Krannich and Ronald L. Krannich (Impact Publications, 1997).

Electronic Resume Revolution: Create a Winning Resume for the New World of Job Seeking. Joyce Lain Kennedy and Thomas J. Morrow (John Wiley & Sons, 1995).

Electronic Resumes: A Complete Guide to Putting Your Resume On-Line. James C. Gonyea and Wayne M. Gonyea (Harvard Business School Press, 1996).

Encyclopedia of Job-Winning Resumes. Myra Fournier and Jeffrey Spin (Round Lake Publishing Co., 1993).

The Enhanced Occupational Outlook Handbook. J. Michael Farr, Laverne L. Ludden, and Paul Mangin, compilers (Jist Works, 1997).

Get Hired! Winning Strategies to Ace the Interview. Paul C. Green (Bard Press, 1996).

Get What You Deserve! How to Guerrilla Market Yourself. Jay Conrad Levinson and Seth Godin (Avon Books, 1997).

How to Get Hired Today! George E. Kent (VGM Career Horizons, 1991).

Negotiating Your Salary: How to Make $1,000 a Minute. Jack Chapman (Ten Speed Press, 1996).

Point and Click Jobfinder. Seth Godin (Dearborn Financial Publishing, 1996).

Resume Pro: The Professional's Guide. Yana Parker (Ten Speed Press, 1993).

The Resume Repair Kit. William S. Frank (Careerlab Books, 1995).

The Three Boxes of Life and How to Get Out of Them: An Introduction to Life-Work Planning. Richard Nelson Bolles (Ten Speed Press, 1978).

Three Steps to Your Right Career: Lifeplan Professional Fulfillment Guide. Gary Joseph (Lifeplan, 1996).

Top Secret Resumes and Cover Letters. Steven Provenzano (Dearborn Financial Publishing, 1996).

The 12 Essential Laws for Getting a Job…and Becoming Indispensable. Tony Zeiss (Thomas Nelson, 1997).

Magazines, Newspapers, and Other Publications

Business Week. 1221 Avenue of the Americas, New York, NY 10020, (800) 635-1200, $49.95/yr., (weekly).

Barron's. 200 Liberty Street, New York, NY 10281, (800) 568-7625, $145/yr., (weekly).

Forbes. 60 Fifth Ave., New York, NY 10011, (800) 888-9896, $59.95/yr., (biweekly).

Fortune. P.O. Box 60001, Tampa, FL 33660, (800) 621-8000, $57/yr., (biweekly).

Hoover's Company Information. 1033 La Posada Dr., Suite 250, Austin, TX 78752, (512) 374-4500, fax: (512) 374-4501, Web site: http://www.hoovers.com, $109.95/yr. for access to Web site.

National Business Employment Weekly. 84 Second Ave., Chicopee, MA 01020, (413) 592-7761, $199/yr., (weekly).

Nation's Business. U.S. Chamber of Commerce Center for Small Business, 1615 H St. NW, Washington, DC 20062, (202) 463-5434, e-mail: ireadnb@nationsbusiness.org, $22/yr., (monthly).

The New York Times. P.O. Box 2047, S. Hackensack, NJ 07606, (800) 631-2500, $374.40/yr., (daily).

Strategy and Business. 114 Mayfield Ave., Edison, NJ 08837, (800) 810-1404, $38/yr., (quarterly).

The Wall Street Journal. 200 Liberty St., New York, NY 10281, (800) 568-7625, $175/yr., (daily).

Online Resources

4work.com, http://www.4work.com

AboutWork! (America Online keyword: AboutWork)

Acron Central, http://www.AcronCentral.com/Prep.htm

America Online Classifieds (keyword: Classified)

America's Employers, http://www.americasemployers.com

America's Job Bank, http://www.ajb.dni.us

AOL Workplace (America Online keyword: Find a Job)

Boldface Jobs, http://www.boldfacejobs.com

BranchOut, http://www.branchout.com

Career City, http://www.careercity.com

Career Exposure, http://www.careerexposure.com

Gonyea Online Career Center (America Online keyword: Career Center or Gonyea)

*CAREER*Magazine, http://www.careermag.com

Career Mosaic, http://www.careermosaic.com

Career Path.com, http://www.careerpath.com

Career Resumes, http://www.branch.com/cr/cr.html

Career Shop, http://www.tenkey.com/cshop

Careers.wsj.com, http://www.careers.wsj.com

Curry Business Systems, Inc., http://www. curryinc.com

DataWay Resources, http://www.sni.net/dataway

Electra, (America Online keyword: Electra)

e.span, http://www.espan.com

GETAJOB, http://www.getajob.com

Hoover's Online, http://www.hoovers.com

Internet Career Connection, http://www.iccweb.com

Interviewing and Networking, (America Online keyword: AboutWork)

JobBank USA, http://www.jobbankusa.com

JobCenter, http://www.jobcenter.com

JobHunt, http://www.job-hunt.org

Job Openings, http://www.tiac.net/users/jobs/req_doc.html

JobSmart, http://jobsmart.org/tools/salary/index.htm

Jobs Through PursuitNet, http://www.tiac.net/users/jobs/index.html

JOBTRAK, http://www.JOBTRAK.com

JobWeb, http://www.jobweb.com

Manpower Technical, http://training.manpower.com

Microsoft Corporation, http://www.microsoft.com/jobs

The Monster Board, http://www.monster.com

NationJob Network, http://www.nationjob.com

NBEW "Talent for Hire", http://www.occ.com/occ/TalentForHire.html

Negotiating Your Salary or Raise (America Online keyword: Find a Job)

Newsgroups, http://www.ub-careers.buffalo.edu/career/news1.html

The Internet's Online Career Center, http://www.occ.com

Ray & Berndtson Online, http://www.prb.com/welcome.html

Recruiters Online Network, http://www.ipa.com

Resumes on the Web, http://www.resweb.com

Resume Publishing Company, http://www.sni.net/cha/trpc.htm

The Riley Guide, http://www.dbm.com/jobguide/

SkillSearch, http://www.skillsearch.com/

TE Inc. Info, http://www.teinc.com/home3.htm

VirtualResume, http://www.webcom.com/vitae/welcome.html

world.hire, http://world.hire.com/index.html

Writing a Resume, http://www.gsia.cmu.edu/afs/andrew/gsia/
coc/student/resume.html

Associations and Organizations

Advocate Career Services. 7676 Hazard Center Dr., Suite 500, San Diego, CA
92108, (800) 542-4048, e-mail: acscenter@aol.com.

A. T. Kearney. 222 W. Adams St., Chicago, IL 60606, (312) 648-0111, fax: (312)
223-6200.

Battalia Winston International. 300 Park Ave., New York, NY 10022, (212) 308-
8080, e-mail: info@battaliawinston.com, Web site: http://battaliawinston.com.

Custom Databanks. 60 Sutton Pl. South, Suite 14BN, New York, NY 10022, (212)
888-1650.

D. F. Foster Partners. 570 Lexington Ave., 14th Floor, New York, NY 10022, (212)
872-6232.

DHR International. Riverside Plaza, Suite 2220, Chicago, IL 60606, (312) 782-
1581.

The Diversified Search Companies. One Commerce Sq., 2005 Market St.,Suite
3300, Philadelphia, PA 19103, (215) 732-6666, fax: (215) 568-8399, e-mail:
diversified@divsearch.com, Web site: http://www.divsearch.com.

Egon Zehnder International. 350 Park Ave., New York, NY 10022, (212) 519-6000, fax: (212) 519 6060, e-mail: EZI-NYC-Research@ezi.net, Web site: http://www.webcom.com/zehnder/index.html.

Gilbert Tweed Associates. 415 Madison Ave., 20th FloorNew York, NY 10017, (212) 758-3000, fax: (212) 832-1040, e-mail: info@gilberttweed.com, Web site: http://gilberttweed.com.

Goodrich & Sherwood. 521 Fifth Ave., New York, NY 10175, (212) 697-4131.

Gould, McCoy & Chadick. 300 Park Ave., New York, NY 10022, (212) 688-8671, fax: (212) 308-4510, Web site: http://www.gouldmccoychadick.com.

Handy HRM. 250 Park Ave., Suite 519, New York, NY, 10177, (212) 557-0400, fax: (212) 557-3531.

Heidrick & Struggles. 245 Park Ave., Suite 4300, New York, NY 10167, (212) 867-9876, fax: (212) 370-9035, Web site: http://www.h-s.com/e_search.htm.

Howe-Lewis International. 521 Fifth Ave., 36th Floor, New York, NY 10175, (212) 697-5000, fax: (212) 697-6600.

Korn/Ferry International. 303 Peachtree St. NE, Suite 1600, Atlanta, GA 30308, (404) 577-7542, fax: (404) 584-9781, Web site: http://www.kornferry.com.ar/intnorte.html.

Lamalie Amrop International. 200 Park Ave., Suite 3100, New York, NY 10166, (212) 953-7900, fax: (212) 953-7907, Web site: http://epe.cornell.edu/cashen.htm.

McCann, Choi & Associates, LLC. 590 Madison Ave., New York, NY 10022, (212) 755-7051.

NACE (National Association of Colleges and Employers). 62 Highland Ave., Bethlehem, PA 18017, (800) 544-5272, fax: (610) 868-0208, Web site: http://www.jobweb.org.

Norman Broadbent. 200 Park Ave., New York, NY 10166, (212) 953-6990, fax: (212) 599-3673, e-mail: info@nb.search.com.

PinPoint Salary Service. 376 Mark Ave., Glendale Hgts., IL 60139, (773) 472-5279, Web site: http://www.members.aol.com/payraises.

Ray & Berndtson. 301 Commerce, Suite 2300, Fort Worth, TX 76102, (817) 334-0500, fax: (817) 334-0779, Web site: http://www.prb.com/welcome.html.

Russell Reynolds Associates. 200 Park Ave., 23rd Floor, New York, NY 10166, (212) 351-2000, fax: (212) 370-0896, e-mail: info@russreyn.com, Web site: http://www.russreyn.com.

Ward Howell. 99 Park Ave. 20th Floor, Suite 2000, New York, NY 10016, (212) 697-3730, fax: (212) 697-1398.

Witt, Keiffer, Ford, Hadelman, Lloyd. 2015 Spring Rd., Oakbrook, IL 60523, (630) 574-5070, fax: (630) 990-1382, Web site: http://www.wittkeiffer.com

INDEX